SpringerBriefs in Computer Science

T0184334

Series Editors
Stan Zdonik
Peng Ning
Shashi Shekhar
Jonathan Katz
Xindong Wu
Lakhmi C Jain
David Padua
Xuemin Shen
Borko Furht

For further volumes:
http://www.springer.com/series/10028

Rafael Silva Pereira · Karin K. Breitman

Video Processing
in the Cloud

 Springer

Rafael Silva Pereira
Webmedia, Globo.com
Rio de Janeiro
Brazil
e-mail: rafaelspereira@gmail.com

Dr. Karin K. Breitman
Department of Informatics
Pontifcia Universidade Catlica do
  Rio de Janeiro
Rio de Janeiro
Brazil
e-mail: karin@inf.puc-rio.br

ISSN 2191-5768
ISBN 978-1-4471-2136-7
DOI 10.1007/978-1-4471-2137-4
Springer London Dordrecht Heidelberg New York

e-ISSN 2191-5776
e-ISBN 978-1-4471-2137-4

British Library Cataloguing in Publication Data
A catalogue record for this book is available from the British Library

Cover design: eStudio Calamar, Berlin/Figueres

Printed on acid-free paper

Springer is part of Springer Science+Business Media (www.springer.com)

The Map Reduce approach, proposed by Dean and Ghemawat [10], is an efficient way for processing very large datasets using a computer cluster and, more recently, cloud infrastructures. Traditional Map Reduce implementations, however, provide neither the necessary flexibility (to choose among different encoding techniques in the mapping stage) nor control (to specify how to organize results in the reducing stage), required to process video files. The Split&Merge tool, presented in this book, generalizes the Map Reduce paradigm, and provides an efficient solution that contemplates relevant aspects of intense processing video applications.

Contents

1 Introduction 1
  1.1 Context 2
  1.2 Goals 3
  1.3 Main Contributions 4

2 Background 5
  2.1 Cloud Computing Paradigms 6
  2.2 Amazon Web Services Platform 8
  2.3 The Map-Reduce Paradigm and Distributed Data Processing ... 11

3 Video Compression 13
  3.1 Image Compression 13
  3.2 Lossless Video Compression 16
  3.3 Lossy Video Compression 17
  3.4 Video Compression for Internet Distribution 20

4 The Split&Merge Architecture 23
  4.1 The Split&Merge for Video Compression 25
    4.1.1 The Split Step 27
    4.1.2 The Process Step 29
    4.1.3 The Merge Step 32
  4.2 Deployment in the AWS Cloud 33
  4.3 Fault Tolerance Aspects 34
  4.4 Performance Tests 35
  4.5 A Cost Analysis 37

5 Case Studies 39
  5.1 The Split&Merge for Globo.com Internet Video Compression ... 39
  5.2 The Split&Merge for Video Event Extraction Using OCR 42

Contents

6 Limitations   49

7 Conclusions   53
   7.1   Future Work   54

Glossary   57

References   59

Index   63

Chapter 1
Introduction

Abstract The volume of information to be processed, allied to seasonal peaks that require extra processing, creates a demand for a high, upfront, infrastructure investment that is often inefficient, because for good portion time, resources end up being idle. In this scenario, providers of on demand computing power in the Cloud–aka Hardware as a Service (HaaS), are becoming increasingly popular. One of the areas where the volume of information to be processed is increasing at a very fast pace is Video Production and Distribution, basically because The Internet brought the potential to completely reinvent the TV. From a technical viewpoint, this reinvention can be translated in huge challenges, including the ability to process, index, store, and distribute nearly limitless amounts of data. This is exactly where the Cloud could play an important role.

Keywords Cloud computing · Internet video · Seasonal demands · On demand computing

As computer systems evolve, the volume of data to be processed increases significantly, either as a consequence of the expanding amount of available information, or due to the possibility of performing highly complex operations that were not feasible in the past. Nevertheless, tasks that depend on the manipulation of large amounts of information are still performed at large computational cost, i.e., either the processing time will be large, or they will require intensive use of computer resources.

In this scenario, the efficient use of available computational resources is paramount, and creates a demand for systems that can optimize the use of resources in relation to the amount of data to be processed. This problem becomes increasingly critical when the volume of information to be processed is variable, i.e., there is a seasonal variation of demand. Such demand variations are caused by a variety of factors, such as an unanticipated burst of client requests, a time-critical simulation, or high volumes of simultaneous video uploads, e.g. as a consequence of a public

R. S. Pereira and K. K. Breitman, *Video Processing in the Cloud*,
SpringerBriefs in Computer Science, DOI: 10.1007/978-1-4471-2137-4_1,

contest. In these cases, there are moments when the demand is very low (resources are almost idle) while, conversely, at other moments, the processing demand exceeds the resources capacity.

Moreover, from an economical perspective, seasonal demands do not justify a massive investment in infrastructure, just to provide enough computing power for peak situations. In this light, the ability to build adaptive systems, capable of using on demand resources provided by Cloud Computing infrastructures [1–3], is very attractive.

1.1 Context

One of the areas where the volume of information to be processed is increasing at a very fast pace is Video Production and Distribution [38]. The increasing popularity of videos on the Internet, allied to the advances in network technology seen in the last decade, is drastically changing TV as we know it. In the past decades there was a very clear distinction among those who produced, distributed, and consumed video contents. Traditionally, video footage was produced by TV channels and by independent companies, distributed to local broadcasters, to then reach general audiences. Roles and responsibilities were clear down the line [31].

A few years ago the "family around the TV set" scenario was greatly challenged, as cable multiplied the number of choices, and hardware prices allowed middle class families to own as many TV sets as there were members in the family. If cable only stretched the model, the Internet has the potential to completely reinvent TV as we know it.

Firstly, because it allows users to see what they want, when they want—suppressing the need for additional hardware. Digital Video Recorders (notably the TiVo) popularized the concept of letting the consumer chose a more convenient time to watch a program. However, with the increase in bandwidth availability for the last mile [39], cable and ASDL [40], it makes much more sense to stream the content directly from the internet than recording it for later use.

Secondly, and much more important, because it removes the barrier that separates producers, distributers and consumers. In the Internet, anyone can produce and distribute high quality content. As a result, there is much more available, making the competition for audiences much tougher, and changing viewing habits in an irreversible fashion.

Thirdly, the Internet allows the mix and match of multi source content. It is becoming commonplace for networks to mix their own footage with User Generated Content (UGC)—to provide a more realistic experience. Recent Haiti earthquake coverage featured as much home made mobile phone videos than proprietary professional footage.

In this scenario, video production and distribution are no longer the privilege of a few. Users were given a front seat, forcing giants to explore new business models. What we see, in fact, is that every day the evolution of technology is challenging established business models, being driven by consumers that require a more complete, flexible and interactive experience.

From a technical point of view, there are also big challenges, which include the ability to process, index, store and distribute very large amounts of data.

Fifty years ago, video was produced in a single format, mostly because its consumption was restricted to some specific screens. Today, however, it is often necessary to generate different versions (encoding and compression) of the same information piece, so one can have access to it on dozens of different devices, such as PC, mobile phones, game consoles, media centers, tablets, PDAs, eBook readers, not to mention router type devices that allow the use of regular TV sets to display Internet content, such as Apple TV, Google TV, BoxeeBox, among others. Such devices offer different hardware capabilities, which often means a different compatibility with media formats and compression profiles. This is a critical problem, as video processing is notably computationally expensive as it is data intensive, time, and resource consuming.

In addiction to the proliferation of different devices, as video technology evolves, it is not uncommon that the market elects preferred platforms for Internet Video distribution. A decade ago RealNetworks's technology RealVideo and RealMedia took the lead, followed by MS Windows Media, Adobe's Flash with the future looking into HTML 5 [41]. Each of these technologies defines a set of associated formats, codecs and transport protocols. Switching video platforms will likely require transcoding contents to new formats, codecs, as well as server migration. For a medium sized content provider, with hundreds of thousands of video files, transcoding all this content, to support this technology evolution, becomes an unprecedented challenge.

Associated with this need for multiple formats, with the increasing of bandwidth availability in last mile, there is also an increasing demand for high quality content, or, specifically, high definition (HD) videos, that requires much more computational resources to be produced, since a HD video may have six times more information than a standard definition (SD) video. Considering that video consumption in the Internet is growing, as well as the demand for higher quality content (HD, 3D), dealing efficiently with transcoding processes is considered very strategic.

In summary, the challenge for video production and distribution companies is to process unprecedented volumes of HD video, and distribute it across several different devices and several different media platforms, which means a significant increasing in the encoding process, and, as consequence, in the time and cost required to perform this task.

1.2 Goals

In *Video Processing in The Cloud* we present an architecture for processing large volumes of video. Our proposal takes advantage of the elasticity provided by Cloud Computing infrastructures. We define elasticity as the ability of a software to provision computational resources needed to perform a particular task on demand. The scope of this work is limited to the range of software applications that have the following characteristics:

- There is a need for processing large volumes of data, i.e., applications where the amount of information to be processed to obtain the desired result is so large that the time required to complete this task using a traditional approach is not acceptable;
- There is a seasonal demand for processing, i.e., there are moments where the amount of information to be processed exceeds the capacity of available resources, while at other times the same resources may be idle;
- Extraordinary and ad hoc situations, where the infrastructure will need to scale up or down repeated times, e.g., transcoding all legacy content from one compression technology to a different one;
- There is a gain in reducing the maximum possible time necessary to obtain the desired result, e.g., immediacy.

1.3 Main Contributions

The main contributions of this research are as follows:

- To propose a general architecture for large scale distributed video processing system, which is capable to address these problems;
- Develop an algorithm that allows parallel and distributed task processing, which takes advantage of the elasticity provided by Cloud platforms, adapting computational resources according to current demands;
- To implement different prototypes to demonstrate the feasibility of the proposed approach;
- To identify and provide a precise formulation of problems characterized by the seasonal demand for large volumes of video processing.

Chapter 2
Background

Abstract To understand how the Cloud could be important for Video processing applications, first we have identify which are the cloud computing characteristics and what are the different Cloud models or layers. It is also fundamental to know which are the available Cloud platforms, and what is possible to implement with the provided services. One of these platforms, the Amazon Web Services, provides several different services that can be combined in order to perform specific tasks, such as intensive processing and massive storage. Since we are talking about processing high volume of information, it is also relevant to analyze the paradigms that could be used in this task. The Map Reduce approach, proposed by Dean and Ghemawat, is an efficient way for processing very large datasets using a computer cluster and, more recently, cloud infrastructures.

Keywords Cloud computing paradigms · Amazon web services · Map-Reduce

Today's web is filled with browser-based applications that are used regularly by millions of users. Some applications have to deal with billions of server requests on a daily basis, and these numbers keep growing. Such applications need to be designed to scale, to expand onto improved and/or additional hardware, and to do this transparently (or at the least without having to take down the application for maintenance). The hardware that a web application runs on is an important component when it comes to dealing with large-scale applications. Applications such as Gmail, YouTube and Flickr that run across thousands of machines are good examples since they require different types of hardware, e.g. web-servers, databases, etc. However, as the number of users grows, the cost to keep the application up and running increases dramatically. The cost for maintenance, physical space, cooling, power, operations, increases for each server that is added to the environment, even if its resources are not fully used.

With very large applications, such as YouTube, that typically have more than two billion videos watched in a month, the costs associated with maintaining the required infrastructure is unpredictable. To manage this infrastructure, there are basically two options:

1. To provide resources based on peak situations, which basically means that, for the most part, resources will be idle;
2. Provide resources based on the average number of requests, which means that in some situations the servers will be overloaded and the quality of service will be affected.

None of the above alternatives is good from a business perspective. The first one is very expensive, as the cost is basically associated with the price of hardware itself, and not with its usage. In the second one, the quality of service may be impacted, and, in the long run, it may signify loss of clients and/or business opportunities.

In this scenario Cloud Computing appears as an interesting alternative, as its "everything as a service" model provides an economically attractive solution to demand variations.

2.1 Cloud Computing Paradigms

For the purpose of this book, Cloud Computing is defined as an Internet-based computing, where there is a large group of interconnected computers (Cloud), that share their resources, software, and information (computing), on demand, according to the user needs [4]. Vaquero et al. attempt to pin down a suitable definition for clouds that describes how they differ from grids. Their proposed definition is thorough, but verbose:

"Clouds are a large pool of easily usable and accessible virtualized resources (such as hardware, development platforms and/or services). These resources can be dynamically reconfigured to adjust to a variable load (scale), allowing also for an optimum resource utilization. This pool of resources is typically exploited by a pay-per-use model in which guarantees are offered by the Infrastructure Provider by means of customized SLAs" [4].

In creating their definition, Vaquero et al. studied definitions from numerous experts, which featured many attributes of cloud computing such as immediate scalability, optimal usage of resources, pay-as-you-go pricing models, and virtualized hardware and software.

Cloud computing is a paradigm shift following the shift from mainframe to client–server in the early 1980s. Details are abstracted from the users, who no longer have need expertise in, or control over, the technology infrastructure "in the cloud" that supports them [5]. Cloud computing describes a new supplement, consumption, and delivery model for IT services based on the Internet, and it typically involves over-the-Internet provision of dynamically scalable and often virtualized resources [6, 7].

Cloud computing infrastructures are typically broken down into three layers [4, 61]: "software", "platform" and "infrastructure". Each layer serves a different purpose and offers different products to businesses and individuals around the world, and, conversely, every layer can be perceived as a customer of the layer below [61].

The Software as a Service (SaaS) layer offers service based on the concept of renting software from a service provider, rather than buying it yourself. It basically refers to providing on-demand applications over the Internet. The software is hosted on centralized network servers and made available over the web or, also, intranet. Also known as "software on demand" it is currently the most popular type of cloud computing by offering high flexibility, enhanced scalability and less maintenance. Yahoo mail, Google docs, Flickr, Google Calendar are all instances of SaaS. With a cloud-based email service, for example, all that one has to do is register and login to the central system to start to send and receive messages. The service provider hosts both the application and data, so the end user is free to use the service from anywhere. SaaS is very effective in lowering the costs of business as it provides the business an access to applications at a cost normally less expensive than a licensed application fee. This is only possible due to its monthly fees based revenue model. With SaaS, users no longer need to worry about installation or upgrades [62].

Platform as a Service (PaaS) offers a development platform for developers. End users write their own code and the PaaS provider uploads that code and presents it on the web. SalesForce.com's is an example of PaaS. PaaS provides services to develop, test, deploy, host and maintain applications in the same integrated development environment. It also provides some level of support for the design of software applications. Thus, PaaS offers a faster and usually cost effective model for software application development and deployment. The PaaS provider manages upgrades, patches and other routine system maintenance. PaaS is based on a metering or subscription model so users only pay for what they use. Users take what they need without worrying about the complexity behind the scenes [42].

There are basically four types of PaaS solutions—*social application platforms, raw compute platforms, web application platforms* and *business application platforms* [43]. Facebook is a type of social application platform wherein third parties can write new applications that are then made available to end users.

The final layer in the cloud computing stack is the infrastructure. Infrastructure as a Service (IaaS) is the process in which computing infrastructure is delivered as a fully outsourced service. Some of the companies that provide infrastructure services are IBM, Amazon.com, among others. Managed hosting and provision of development environments are the services included in the IaaS layer. The user can buy the infrastructure according to his or her requirements at any particular point of time, instead of buying an infrastructure that may not be used for months. IaaS operates on a "Pay as you go" model, ensuring that the users pay for only what they are using. Virtualization enables IaaS providers to offer almost unlimited instances of servers to customers, and make use of the hosting hardware cost-effective. IaaS users enjoy access to enterprise grade IT Infrastructure and resources, that might be very costly if otherwise purchased. Thus, dynamic scaling, usage based pricing, reduced costs and access to premium IT resources are some of the benefits of IaaS. IaaS is also sometimes referred to as Hardware as a Service (HaaS). An Infrastructure as a Service offering also provides maximum flexibility because just about anything that can be virtualized can be run on these platforms. This is perhaps the biggest benefit of an IaaS environment. For a startup or small business, one of the most difficult things to do is keep capital expenditures under control. By moving the computational infrastructure to the cloud, one has the ability to scale up and down as needed.

In next section, we detail the Amazon Web Services Cloud Platform, as well as its main services, that provided the basic infrastructure for the video processing architecture presented in this book.

2.2 Amazon Web Services Platform

Amazon Web Services (AWS) [48] is a group of cloud-based services provided by Amazon that differs from traditional hosting since its resources are charged by actual usage. These services provide cloud-based computation, storage and other functionality that enable organizations and individuals to deploy applications and services on an on-demand basis and at commodity prices [61]. The AWS platform is composed by several services that complement one another. Elastic Compute Cloud (EC2), for processing, the Simple Storage Service (S3), for binary storage, SimpleDB, for structured data storage, Relational Database Service (RDS), for relational databases, Cloud Front, for content delivery, are examples of such services. For the purposes of this project, EC2 and S3 are the most relevant services.

Amazon EC2 is a web service interface that provides resizable computing capacity in the cloud. Based on IaaS model, it allows a complete control of computing resources and reduces the time required to obtain and boot new server instances. Users of EC2 can launch and terminate server instances on a matter of minutes, as opposed to delays of several hours, days or weeks, typical of traditional hardware solutions. This feature is particularly interesting because it allows applications to quickly scale up and down their processing resources, as computing requirements change, while in the traditional hardware approach, it can take several weeks or even months to get a new server running.

Amazon EC2 provides developers with two APIs for interacting with the service, allowing intances administration operations, such as start, stop, reboot, query information, etc. One is the Query API in which operations send data using GET or POST methods over HTTP or HTTPS. The other is the SOAP [46] API in which operations send data using SOAP 1.1 over HTTPS.

The main concept behind EC2 is that of a server instances [8]. There are a number of different types of instances that users can choose from, divided into six categories: standard, micro, high-memory, high-CPU, cluster and cluster-GPU.

Each type has several subtypes, with various levels of processing power, memory and storage, and users can choose between them according their needs.

Because AWS is built on top of heterogeneous hardware processing power, a standard measure Amazon EC2 Compute Units is used. One EC2 Compute Unit provides the equivalent CPU capacity of a 1.0–1.2 GHz 2007 Opteron or 2007 Xeon processor [9].

The storage provided on an instance (referred to by Amazon as "instance storage") is volatile. Data will survive the instance rebooting, either intentionally or accidentally, but it will not survive an underlying hard drive failing or an instance being terminated. It is also possible to choose a non-volatile storage for the instance, called Elastic Block Storage (EBS). Amazon EBS allows users to create storage volumes from 1 GB to 1 TB that can be mounted as devices by Amazon EC2 instances. Multiple volumes can be mounted to the same instance. Using an EBS as instance storage, users can temporally stop their instances, without data loss.

The EC2 Instances are created by launching machine images known as Amazon Machine Images (AMI) [47], which contain the operating system that will be launched on the instance, along with software applications and their configuration. AMIs are stored on Amazon S3 and Amazon provides a number of pre-bundled public AMIs (with Linux, UNIX or Windows as the OS), that can be immediately launched by users, and do not require specific configuration.

Users can also create their own custom AMIs (private AMIs), either from scratch or using a public AMI as base. Private AMIs are created by a process called bundling, in which a machine image is compressed, encrypted and split, the parts of which are then uploaded to Amazon S3.

EC2 provides the ability to place instances in multiple locations. EC2 locations are composed of Regions and Availability Zones. Regions consist of one or more Availability Zones, are geographically dispersed. Availability Zones are distinct locations that are engineered to be insulated from failures in other Availability Zones and provide inexpensive, low latency network connectivity to other Availability Zones in the same Region [61].

The Amazon S3 service provides a simple web service interface that can be used to store and retrieve data on the web, and provides a scalable data storage infrastructure [70]. It is designed to make storing and retrieving data on AWS as simple as possible. Data is stored using a straightforward flat model, on top of which users can build their own storage structures using hierarchies. S3 also features a simple, yet versatile, access control system, where objects can be made private, public or be made accessible by certain groups of users.

The two main concepts of S3 are buckets and objects [61]. Buckets are containers for data objects. All objects stored on S3 are stored in buckets. An object consists of four components: a value (the data being stored in that object), a key (the unique identifier for that object), metadata (additional data associated with the object) and an access control policy.

Each bucket has a name that is completely unique within S3. Bucket names are directly mapped to URLs for addressing data stored on S3. If a bucket is named *cloudencoding* then it can be addressed with the URL http://cloudencoding.s3. amazonaws.com. This URL can be appended with the name of an object to create an address for any object stored on S3.

The other main concept of S3 is an object. Object sizes vary from one byte to five gigabytes. There is no limit to the number of objects that a user can store on S3 and no limit to the number of objects that can be stored in a bucket. A bucket can be stored in one of several Regions. Users can choose a Region to optimize latency, minimize costs, or address regulatory requirements [61, 70].

S3 objects are redundantly stored on multiple devices across multiple facilities in an Amazon S3 Region. To help ensure durability, Amazon S3 PUT and COPY operations synchronously store your data across multiple facilities before returning. Once stored, Amazon S3 maintains the durability of your objects by quickly detecting and repairing any lost redundancy. Amazon S3 also regularly verifies the integrity of data stored using checksums. If corruption is detected, it is repaired using redundant data. In addition, Amazon S3 calculates checksums on all network traffic to detect corruption of data packets when storing or retrieving data [70].

The key is the name of the object and must be absolutely unique within the bucket that contains the object. Keys can be any size from one byte to 1,024 bytes. Keys can be listed by their bucket and a prefix. This allows users to use common prefixes to group together their objects into a hierarchy, meaning that the flat storage model of S3 buckets can then be turned into a directory-like model for storing data. Object keys can also be given suffixes, like *.jpeg* or *.mpeg*, to help make the key more.

The metadata of an object is a set of key/value pairs and is divided into two types: system metadata and user metadata. System metadata is used by S3 while user metadata can be any key/value pair defined by the user. User metadata keys and values can be any length, as long as the total size of all metadata (system and user) for an object is less than two kilobytes.

Access control on objects is managed by access control lists (ACL). Every object, as well as every bucket, has an ACL. When a request is made to S3, it checks the ACL of the object or bucket to check if the requester has been granted permission. If the requester is not authorized to access the object then an error is returned by S3. There are a number of different types of groups that can be granted permissions and a number of different permissions, such as READ, WRITE and FULL CONTROL.

S3 provides two APIs for making requests, the first uses a REST protocol and the second uses SOAP. The REST API uses standard HTTP headers and status codes, with some additional headers added in by S3 to increase functionality.

Amazon S3 also has the option of the Reduced Redundancy Storage (RRS) that enables customers to reduce their costs by storing non-critical, reproducible data at lower levels of redundancy than Amazon S3's standard storage. It provides a cost-effective solution for distributing or sharing content that is durably stored elsewhere, or for storing thumbnails, transcoded media, or other processed data that can be easily reproduced. The RRS option stores objects on multiple devices across multiple facilities, providing 400 times the durability of a typical disk drive, but does not replicate objects as many times as standard Amazon S3 storage, and thus is even more cost effective [70].

The Amazon AWS Platform also provides several additional services, as previously mentioned, which are not the focus of this research. One of them is the Elastic Map-Reduce, an implementation of Map-Reduce [10] algorithm built on top of the basic AWS infrastructure blocks (EC2 and S3). This feature is particularly interesting because EC2 and S3 alone, are not sufficient to provide efficient and scalable high performance processing architecture. To achieve these goals, one has to build applications that are able to take advantage of the characteristics of IaaS infrastructures, for example, the ability to automatically start and stop machines according to processing demands, or the ability to use several machines to simultaneously process parts of a content. One paradigm that deals with these issues is the Map-Reduce, detailed in the following section.

2.3 The Map-Reduce Paradigm and Distributed Data Processing

The distribution of tasks in a cluster for parallel processing is not a new concept, and there are several techniques that use this idea to optimize the processing of information [49–51]. The Map-Reduce paradigm [10], for example, is a framework for processing large datasets of certain kinds of distributable problems, that makes use of a large number of computers (nodes), collectively referred to as a cluster. It consists of an initial Map stage, where a master node takes the input, chops it into smaller sub-problems, and distributes the parts to worker nodes, which process the information independently; following there is the Reduce stage, where the master node collects the solutions to all the sub-problems and combines them in order to produce the job output. The process is illustrated in Fig. 2.1.

A popular Map-Reduce implementation is Apache's Hadoop [11], which consists of one Job Tracker, to which client applications submit Map-Reduce jobs. The Job Tracker pushes work out to available Task Tracker nodes in the cluster, which execute the map and reduce tasks.

Despite being a very appealing and efficient technique for processing large volumes of data, there are a number of challenges and shortcomings associated with the deployment of Map-Reduce architectures [46]. The first of them is the required infrastructure. To make the process truly effective, one needs several machines acting as nodes, which often requires a large upfront investment in infrastructure. This point is extremely critical in situations where the processing demand is seasonal. In addition, fault tolerance issues and the need of a shared file system to support mappers and reducers make the deployment of a Map-Reduce architecture complex and costly.

To understand how Map-Reduce could be useful to improve the efficiency of a video processing task, and, which of its characteristics we must preserve while building a high performance video processing architecture based on a Cloud

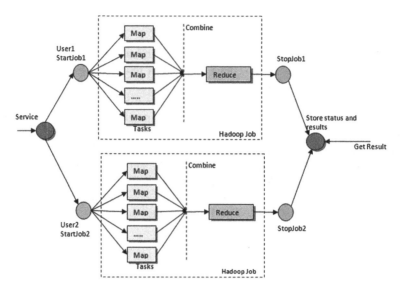

Fig. 2.1 The Map Reduce Architecture [44]

platform, we first need to understand how video compression works, and which are the main steps of this process. Only then, can we discuss the required changes and adaptations to the Map-Reduce paradigm.

In the next chapter, we present a brief introduction to sequential video processing, followed by a discussion on the requirements for parallel video processing, and the required adaptations to the Map-Reduce paradigm so that it serves this specific purpose.

Chapter 3
Video Compression

Abstract The volume of information required to represent a high quality Digital Video is usually very large, which becomes a challenge for Internet distribution of high volumes of content. This is basically why the data must be compressed. A well understanding about this compression process is key to develop new approaches to increase its time efficiency.

Keywords Digital image · Digital video · Video compression · Internet video

Digital video communication today is present in many application scenarios, such as broadcasting, internet video streaming, video capture, among others. Central to all is the communication challenge of conveying source data with the highest possible fidelity within an available bit rate, or, alternatively, conveying source data using the lowest possible bit rate, while maintaining specific reproduction fidelity. In either case, there is fundamental tradeoff between bit rate and fidelity.

The fact is that digital video takes up a lot of space. Uncompressed footage from a camcorder takes up about 17 MB per second of video. Because it takes up so much space, video must be compressed before it is put on the web. To better understand what is a digital video, why it is necessary to perform a data compression on it and why this process is so computational expensive, lets start from the basics of video composition.

3.1 Image Compression

A digital image or a frame of digital video typically consists of three rectangular arrays of integer-valued samples, one array for each of the three components of a tristimulus color representation for the spatial area represented in the image. Image coding often uses a color representation having three components called Y, Cb,

R. S. Pereira and K. K. Breitman, *Video Processing in the Cloud*,
SpringerBriefs in Computer Science, DOI: 10.1007/978-1-4471-2137-4_3,
© Rafael Silva Pereira 2011

$$\begin{bmatrix} 52 & 55 & 61 & 66 & 70 & 61 & 64 & 73 \\ 63 & 59 & 55 & 90 & 109 & 85 & 69 & 72 \\ 62 & 59 & 68 & 113 & 144 & 104 & 66 & 73 \\ 63 & 58 & 71 & 122 & 154 & 106 & 70 & 69 \\ 67 & 61 & 68 & 104 & 126 & 88 & 68 & 70 \\ 79 & 65 & 60 & 70 & 77 & 68 & 58 & 75 \\ 85 & 71 & 64 & 59 & 55 & 61 & 65 & 83 \\ 87 & 79 & 69 & 68 & 65 & 76 & 78 & 94 \end{bmatrix}$$

Fig. 3.1 The 8 × 8 array of Luma with 8 bits of resolution [65]

and Cr [16]. Component Y is called luma and represents brightness, as shown in Fig. 3.1. The two chroma components Cb and Cr represent the extent to which the color deviates from gray toward blue and red, respectively. Because the human visual system is more sensitive to luma than chroma, often a sampling structure is used in which the chroma component arrays each have only one-fourth as many samples as the corresponding luma component array (half the number of samples in both the horizontal and vertical dimensions). This is called 4:2:0 sampling [16]. The amplitude of each component is typically represented with 8 bit of precision per sample for consumer-quality video, which means that every pixel from each component could assume values from 0 to 255.

Based on this structure, a raw image file with 1980 × 1024 spatial resolution, has more than two million pixels for each component, a total of 5.8 MB of data. For an isolated image, it is not too much data. However, for a composition of dozens of images, the size of data becomes an issue, specially if these images will be transmitted over a network. In this scenario, we must reduce the volume of data to be sent. This process is known as compression.

The basic image compression process, used in JPEG [63, 64] standard, can be summarized by the following steps [16]. The compression process is also illustrated in Fig. 3.2:

1. The representation of the colors in the image is converted from RGB to the YCbCr format, that consists of one luma component (Y), representing brightness, and two chroma components, (Cb and Cr), representing color.
2. The resolution of the chroma data is reduced, usually by a factor of 2. This is called subsampling and reflects the fact that the eye is less sensitive to fine color details than to fine brightness details.
3. The image is then splited into blocks of 8 × 8 pixels. For each block, each of the Y, Cb, and Cr data components undergoes a discrete cosine transform (DCT). A DCT is similar to a Fourier transform in the sense that it produces a spatial frequency spectrum.
4. The amplitudes of the frequency components are quantized. Human vision is much more sensitive to small variations in color or brightness over large areas

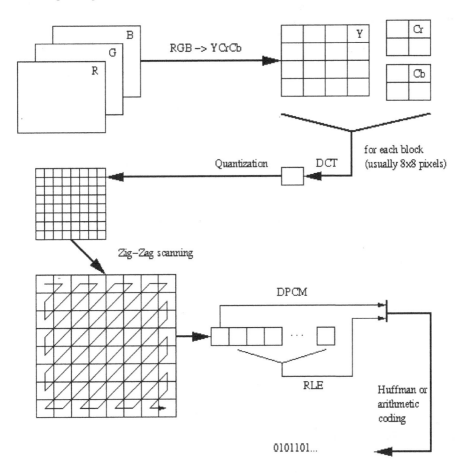

Fig. 3.2 Image compression steps [66]

than to the strength of high-frequency brightness variations. Therefore, the magnitudes of the high-frequency components are stored with a lower accuracy than the low-frequency components. The quality setting of the encoder (e.g. 50 or 95 on a scale of 0–100 in the Independent JPEG Group's library [12]) affects the extent to what the resolution of each frequency component is reduced to. If an excessively low quality setting is used, the high-frequency components are altogether discarded.

5. The resulting data for all 8×8 blocks is further compressed using a lossless algorithm. Lossless algorithms allows for the reconstruction of the exact original data from the compressed data. Examples are the Huffman [52] algorithm or Lempel–Ziv–Welch Coding [53, 54].

The compression ratio can be adjusted according to need by changing the divisors used in the quantization phase. More aggressive divisors means a greater

Fig. 3.3 An image with
successively more
compression ratios from left
to right [65]

compression ratio. Ten to one compression usually results in an image that cannot be distinguished by the naked eye from the original one. One hundred to one compression is usually possible, but will look distinctly distorted compared to the original. The appropriate level of compression depends on the use to which the image will be put to.

Figure 3.3, illustrates how the compression ratio affects the final quality of the decoded image. This occurs due to the quantization step, which introduces losses that can not be recovered by the decoding process. Therefore this compression process was baptized lossy compression. On the other hand, if we suppress the quantization step from the compression process, we can fully reconstruct the original image after decoding, which results in a lossless compression.

3.2 Lossless Video Compression

Digital video comprises a series of digital images, which in the context of video are called frames. Frames are displayed in rapid succession at a constant rate. We measure the rate at which frames are displayed in frames per second (FPS).

The greater the amount of frames per second in a video, the greater will the volume of data required to represent it be. However, reducing the number of frames as a means to reduce the amount of data in a video is not a good compression solution, as the smaller is the amount of frames per second, the worse will the perception of continuity between the images displayed sequentially be. In practice, it is used rates of 20–30 frames per second to represent a video.

The need for video compression arises with the need to store and transmit such information over a given medium, e.g. networks. A 30 frames per second video, with the spatial resolution of 320 × 240 pixels, and a color resolution of 8 bits per pixel, results in a file of approximately 52 Mbps, which makes it virtually impossible to transmit it over the current internet network infrastructure in many countries.

Because digital video is a sequence of images displayed continuously, one way of compressing it is simply compressing each picture separately. This is how much of the compression research started in the mid-1960s [13, 14]. This process basically consists in performing a lossless image compression over each single frame of the video, and it is defined by the MJPEG standard [16, 67].

In general, in the lossless compression process, each image or frame is compressed individually, without taken into consideration the redundancy between subsequent frames. Moreover, in this process the quantization step is not usually performed, i.e. each frame goes through a process of lossless compression, as described in the previous session.

This basic model is very inefficient with respect to compression ratios. If we consider high-definition videos, with bigger spatial resolution and higher frame rates, it is necessary to find an approach in which to explore further characteristics of the video, so as to have a satisfactory reduction in data volume, without deterioration in the quality of the contents.

3.3 Lossy Video Compression

We define lossy video compression, as the process by which the original video is irreparably distorted during the compression process. As the result of the lossy compression process it becomes impossible to rebuild the original file in the decoding. Lossy compression is usually required in order to achieve increased compression ratios, not feasible when using a lossless process. In this process, parts of the original data are discarded in order to drastically reduce the amount of bits needed to represent it. Ideally this is done without introducing significant distortion. In the case of videos, much of the discarded information is not perceptible to the eyes, which makes this process a good alternative to the lossless compression process. However, when compression ratios become very aggressive, it is possible to identify a very significant degradation, which can ultimately turn the contents unrecognizable.

Most modern codec's such as H.264 [17], VP8 [68], WMV, etc. are heavily based on lossy compression algorithms.

To perform a lossy video compression process, most encoders explore two of the video's striking features: spatial and temporal redundancy. Because each video frame can be treated as an isolated image, image compression techniques can be applied directly over them, which will act to reduce spatial redundancy, taking advantage of the correlation between adjacent pixels to reduce the number of bits needed to represent each frame. As to the process of image compression, it is possible to include a quantization step in the compression process of each frame, which will reduce the amount of symbols needed to represent the information through the approximation of similar values. Once down this path, the original values can no longer be recovered, which result in the insertion of irreparable distortions in the content. As mentioned earlier, the larger the quantization step,

Fig. 3.4 The I-frames,
P-frames and B-frames

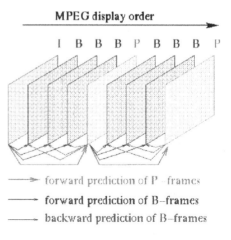

the greater the distortions will be visible on the frames. Typically these can be identified through the formation of small blocks in images, as illustrated by Fig. 3.3.

Furthermore, much of the depicted scene is essentially just repeated in picture after picture without significant changes, so video can be represented more efficiently by sending only the changes to the video scene, rather than coding all regions repeatedly. We refer to such techniques as inter-picture or inter coding. The ability to use temporal redundancy to improve coding efficiency is what fundamentally distinguishes video compression from the intra frame compression process exemplified above.

The basic method of inter compression is to calculate the prediction error between corresponding blocks in the current and previous frames. The error values are then sent to the compression process. Compressed frames generated using prediction are usually called P-frames. When we use both previous and future frames as the reference, the frame is called B-frame (bidirectional frame), as shown in Fig. 3.4.

In motion compensation, depicted in Fig. 3.5, is the process by which each image frame is divided into a fixed number of, usually, square blocks. For each block in the frame, a search is made in the reference frame over the area of the image that allows for the maximum translation that the coder can support. The search is for the best matching block, to give the least prediction error, usually minimizing either the mean square difference, or the mean absolute difference, easier to compute. Typical block sizes are in the order of 16×16 pixels, and the maximum displacement might be around 64 pixels from a block's original position. Several search strategies are possible, most use some kind of sampling mechanism. The most straightforward approach is exhaustive search.

An example of the block structure generated in order to perform a motion compensation is exemplified by Fig. 3.6, that borrows from the MPEG-4 test

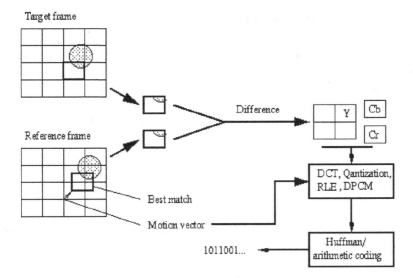

Fig. 3.5 Motion compensation [66]

Fig. 3.6 Motion vectors in a video frame

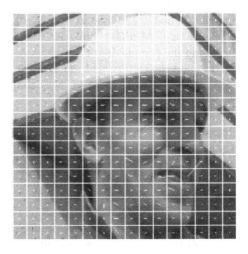

sequence known as "Foreman"[1] [55]. Note that the stationary background is represented by a large numbers of blocks with very similar motion vectors (represented by the short lines starting from each block centre).

---

[1] The Foreman sequence, available publicly, shows closeup of a talking man followed by a camera panning and view of a building being constructed, and is commonly used by ITU-T Video Coding Experts Group for video processing tests.

3.4 Video Compression for Internet Distribution

Internet video distribution is not a new process, however, it has become more and more popular in the past few years, mainly as consequence of improvements in connectivity and bandwidth. Although there's been a significant increase in available bandwidth, the Internet today has a limited capacity to efficiently transfer content in situations where higher data rates are required, e.g. uncompressed video. To allow for the exchange of video content using a common Internet connection, the information must be compressed to low data rates, preferably in the order of a few kilobits per second. The first popular solution for this process was developed by Real Networks, in 1997, with RealVideo, based on H.263 [57] video codec, which delivered a video with no more than a 28.8 Kbps dial-up connection to the Internet.

As time went by, new and better compression algorithms became available, allowing better quality at a lower bitrates. In the past few years, Internet video compression technology has been converging around the H.264/AVC compression standard [17], which is one of the existing *codecs* with highest compression ratio efficiency.

The intent of the H.264/AVC project was to create a standard capable of providing good video quality, at substantially lower bit rates, than previous standards, e.g. MPEG-2 [56], H.263 [57], or MPEG-4 Part 2 [58], without increasing the complexity of design. A design excessively complex would render this solution impractical and too expensive to implement. The standardization of the first version of H.264/AVC was completed in May 2003, has become ever more popular since then.

The evolution of video compression for Internet distribution is a constantly changing scenario, where the dominating technology is always being replaced. It started with RealVideo, which was the most popular technology from 1997 to 2004. In this year Microsoft's Windows Media Services took its place with the new WMV9 codec, that introduced a new process by which to obtain significantly better video compression quality. This technology rapidly became the most popular technology for Internet video, forcing those using Real's solution to migrate to Microsoft's platform. However, with the prioritization of Windows Vista project, Microsoft stopped the evolution of their media platform, which allowed Adobe to develop a similar platform and compete for this market. Adobe, however, did not have a good video compression standard (Sorenson Spark [59]). To make their product more attractive, they focused on user experience and integration of the player inside web pages [60].

With this approach, Adobe's Flash Media platform called the attention of a startup called YouTube, in 2005, which decided to adopt Adobe's technology as their video platform. With the popularization of Internet video, due in a great part to the YouTube phenomena, the Flash Media Platform started to gain market against Microsoft's technology, and became the dominant Internet video technology.

To improve video quality, Adobe added H.264 support to their Flash Player in 2007, and, since then, it became the de facto standard for video on the web.

Analyzing the evolution of Internet video technology, we highlight the constant change in video compression standards. This short history is relevant to the work presented here because for every format/standard change, all legacy content must be re-encoded so that it complies to new standard. This fact has a great impact to large broadcasters, who are forced to transcode very large amounts of video at a large cost to convert their legacy collections. In addition, this process is usually quite complex, time consuming, resource demanding, and very slow.

One last observation is that Internet video consumption is no longer restricted to the computers or web browsers. Today there is a proliferation of devices with playback video capabilities, and different video format support. This means that it is usually the case that a single video needs be transcoded several times, to ensure compatibility with different devices. Worst, of all, legacy content must also be transcoded every time a new device, with a new supported format, is put into the market.

Content producers, from an economical point of view, have little interest to invest in a large transcoding infrastructure. Firstly, because they do not know when a new format will become popular, and, secondly, because they only need to perform the transcoding process once a new format comes in the market. If they invest in a large hardware infrastructure, capable of handling transcoding jobs, chances are the resources will remain idle a great part of the time.

On demand resource allocation made possible by the Cloud, on the other hand, fits perfectly in this scenario, as it allows for the provision of computer processing and storage capabilities according to current needs. When no longer needed, such resources are released.

Based on this, the ability to process video efficiently in a Cloud environment becomes strategic for media production companies. This is the focus of this research. In the following chapter we detail the proposed architecture, showing how it can take advantage when deployed in a Cloud platform.

Chapter 4
The Split&Merge Architecture

Abstract In this chapter, we present the Split&Merge architecture, that explores on demand computing paradigms to rationalize the use of resources. The architecture generalizes the Map-Reduce paradigm, combining it to a provisioning component that dynamically launches virtual machines in private clusters or in the Cloud, and provides an efficient solution that contemplates relevant aspects of intense processing video applications.

Keywords Split&Merge · Map-Reduce · Video compression · Cloud computing · Service oriented architectures · Distributed computing

Scalable and fault tolerant architectures that allow distributed and parallel processing of large volumes of data in Cloud environments are becoming increasingly more desirable as they ensure the needed flexibility and robustness to deal with large datasets more efficiently. We are interested in architectures that deal with video processing tasks, as they are not fully addressed by existing techniques for high performance video processing. In what follows we discuss the requirements for such an architecture, focusing in the dynamic deployment of additional computer resources, as a means to handle seasonal peak loads.

The first point we need to address is flexibility. We want the ability to deploy the proposed architecture on different commercial Cloud platforms. Therefore, the architecture must be simple, componentized, and able to run on a hybrid processing structure, that combines machines in a private cluster with resources available in the Cloud. With this approach it would be possible, for example, to have servers in a local cluster, as well as instances on a public Cloud environment, e.g. Amazon EC2, simultaneously processing tasks. Alternatively, all the processing can be done on servers in a private cluster, but, using a storage in the Cloud.

To make this possible, all components of the architecture should be service oriented, that is, they must implement web services that allow functional

R. S. Pereira and K. K. Breitman, *Video Processing in the Cloud*,
SpringerBriefs in Computer Science, DOI: 10.1007/978-1-4471-2137-4_4,
© Rafael Silva Pereira 2011

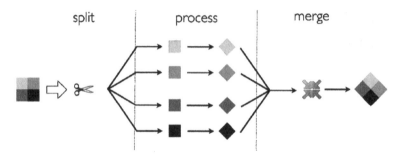

Fig. 4.1 The split, process and merge concept

architectural building-blocks to be accessible over standard Internet protocols, independently of platform, and/or programming languages. This is a key feature when dealing with services in the Cloud. In the case of Cloud services provided by Amazon, for example, it is possible to manipulate data stored in Amazon S3, or even to provision resources in the Amazon EC2, enabling the scaling up or down using programs that communicate through REST web services [15]. Thus, an architecture for task processing should provide a service-oriented interface for scheduling and manipulating jobs. The same paradigm must be used to support the communication among internal components. This makes deployment more flexible, facilitates the extension of existing features, and the addition and/or removal of software components, as needed.

If we analyze the Map-Reduce paradigm [10] in its essence, we note that process optimization is achieved by distributing tasks among available computing resources. It is precisely this characteristic that we want to preserve in the proposed architecture. The possibility of breaking an input, and processing its parts in parallel, is the key to reducing overall processing times [31].

With a focus on these issues, the proposed Split&Merge architecture borrows from key Map-Reduce concepts, to produce a simple, and yet general, infrastructure in which to deal with distributed video processing. The intuition behind it is the straightforward split-distribute-process-merge process illustrated in Fig. 4.1. Similarly to Map-Reduce, this architecture efficiently uses available computing resources.

It is important to note that the proposed architecture was developed with the care to maintain a choice among techniques used in the split, distribute, process and merge steps, so that their implementation can be switched and customized as needed. That secures flexibility, adaptation, extensibility and the accommodation of different applications. In the case of video processing, it is paramount to allow for a choice among different codecs, containers, audio streams, and video splitting techniques. Let us take the case where the input video has no temporal compression, the MJPEG standard [16, 67] for example, as an illustration. In this case, the split can be performed at any frame. Conversely, cases where the input is a video encoded using only p-frame temporal compression, e.g., H.264 [17] Baseline Profile, we must identify the key-frames before splitting.

The generalization of this idea, lead to an architecture in which it is possible to isolate and diversify the implementation for the split, distribute, process and merge steps.

4.1 The Split&Merge for Video Compression

As discussed in Chap. 3, video compression refers to reducing the quantity of data used to represent digital video images, and is a combination of spatial image compression and temporal motion compensation. Video applications require some form of data compression to facilitate storage and transmission. Digital video compression is one of the main issues in digital video encoding, enabling efficient distribution and interchange of visual information.

The process of high quality video encoding is usually very costly to the encoder, and requires a lot of production time. When we consider situations where there are large volumes of digital content, this is even more critical, since a single video may require the server's processing power for long time periods. Moreover, there are cases where the speed of publication is critical. Journalism and breaking news are typical applications in which the time-to-market the video is very short, so that every second spent in video encoding may represent a loss of audience.

Figure 4.2 shows the speed of encoding of a scene, measured in frames per second, with different implementations of the H.264 compression standard [17]. We note that the higher the quality, i.e., the bitrate of the video output, the lower the speed of encoding.

In order to speed up encoding times, there are basically two solutions. The first one is to augment the investment in encoding hardware infrastructure, to be used in full capacity only at peak times. The downside is that probably the infrastructure will be idle a great deal of the remaining time. The second solution is to try and optimize the use of available resources. The ideal scenario is to optimize resources by distributing the tasks among them evenly. In the specific case of video encoding, one approach is to break a video into several pieces and distribute the encoding of each piece among several servers in a cluster. The challenge of this approach is to split, as well as merge video fragments without any perceptible degradation as a consequence of this process.

As described in the previous session, there are several techniques whose goal is to perform parallel and distributed processing of large volumes of information, such as the Map-Reduce paradigm. However, video files possess characteristics that hinder the direct application of distributed processing techniques, without first adjusting the way they deal with the information contained in the video. Firstly we must remark that a video file is a combination of an audio and a video stream,

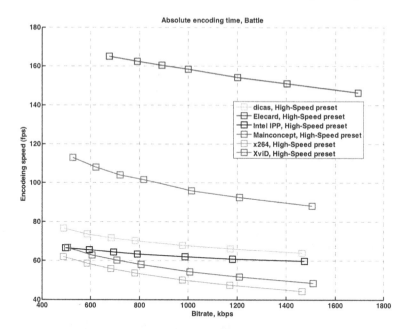

Fig. 4.2 Encoding speed for different H.264 implementations [69]

which should be compressed in separate and using different algorithms. These processes, however, must be done interdependently, so that the final result is decoded in a synchronized way. This means that the video container must maintain the alignment between the two streams (audio and video) at all times. In addition, a video stream can be decomposed into sets of frames, which are strongly correlated, especially in relation to its subsequent frames. In fact, it is the correlation among the frames that allows the reduction of temporal redundancy in certain codecs [17, 58].

Therefore, without adaptation, the Map-Reduce approach is of very little use to video compression. Firstly, a classical Map Reduce implementation would divide the tasks using a single mapping strategy. Video encoding requires that we use different strategies to compressing video and audio tracks. Secondly, the traditional Map-Reduce approach does not take into consideration the order, much less the correlation of the pieces processed by individual units processing different parts of the video. Video encoding requires that we take into consideration frame correlation, and more importantly, the order of frames.

With a focus on these issues, the proposed architecture provides an infrastructure to deal with video processing. That is, for every video received, it is fragmented, its fragments are processed in a distributed environment, and finally, the result of processing is merged. As in the Map-Reduce, this architecture is able to efficiently use the computing resources available, and furthermore, it allows the use of more complex inputs, or more specific processing.

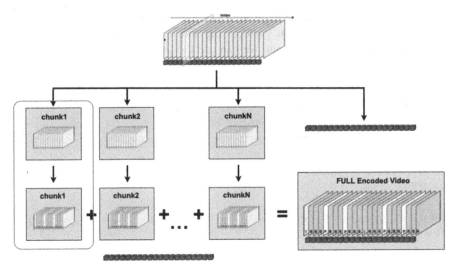

Fig. 4.3 The proposed Split&Merge approach for video compression

4.1.1 The Split Step

In what follows we describe a technique for reducing video encoding times, based on distributed processing over cluster or Cloud environments, implemented using the Split&Merge architecture and illustrated in Fig. 4.3. The fragmentation of media files and the distribution of encoding tasks in a cluster consists in a solution for increasing the performance of encoding, and an evolution of the simple distribution of single complete video encoding tasks in a cluster or Cloud. The idea is to break a media file into smaller files so that its multiple parts can be processed simultaneously on different machines, thereby reducing the total encoding time of the video file. Furthermore, to avoid synchronization problems between audio and video, we must separate the two, so that they can be independently compressed. If processed together, chunks containing both audio and video may generate various synchronization problems, since audio frames do not necessarily have the same temporal size than video frames. One should thus avoid processing both streams together, for it may generate audible glitches, delays and undesirable effects. Because the overall impact to the performance is very small, the audio stream is processed in one piece (no fragmentation).

The greatest challenge of video processing, differently from text files, is that it is not possible to split a video file anywhere. If the input video already provides some form of temporal compression, then it would be necessary to first identify its key-frames, so that the cuts are made at their exact positions. This is necessary because in the case where there is temporal compression, some frames (b-frames and p-frames) require information existing on key-frames to be decoded. Thus, a separation of video chunks, when there is temporal compression, which isolates a b-frame or p-frame from the key-frame required for its decoding, would derail the process of transcoding. To perform the video stream split, considering a temporal compression in the input, we can use the following algorithm:

identify key-frames
open **chunk**
for each **frame** *in input video*
    if **frame** *is key-frame and chunkSize > **GOP***
        add **frame** *to* **chunk**
        close **chunk**
        open new **chunk**
    end
    add **frame** *to* **chunk**
end
close **chunk**

Situations where the original video does not show temporal compression, are special cases where the video can be split at specific frame numbers or at regular intervals. The important point here is to ensure that no frame coexists in more than one chunk, and that no frame is lost. In the cases where there is temporal compression, the duplicated key-frames should be discarded in the merge step.

A key point in the fragmentation of the input video is to determine the size of the chunks to be generated. This decision is closely related with the output that should be generated, that is, the video codec and compression parameters passed to it in the processing step. This is because, after processing, the chunks will present a key-frame in its beginning and in the end. Indiscriminate chunk fragmentation will produce an output video with an excess of key-frames, reducing the efficiency of compression, as key-frame typically contains much more information than a, b or p frame. To illustrate this fact, it is frequent the use of 250 frames in between consecutive key-frames (GOP size), for a typical 29.97 fps video. Thus, if in the split step chunks are generated with less than 250 frames, the efficiency of the temporal compression of the encoder will be inevitably reduced. A good approach is to perform the split so that the number of chunks generated is equal to the number of nodes available for processing. However, when we use an elastic processing structure, we can further optimize this split, analyzing what is the optimum amount of chunks to be generated, which certainly varies according to the duration of the video, and the characteristics of the input, and output to be produced.

This optimized split would require the implementation of a decision-making algorithm to evaluate the characteristics of input and output, choosing what size of fragment will use resources more efficiently, producing a high quality result and with acceptable response times. The implementation of this algorithm is quite desirable in order to improve the efficiency of the process, however, it is beyond the scope of this work.

When we split a video file into several chunks, or smaller files, we must repair their container, i.e., rewrite the header and trailer, so that the input chunks could be completely decoded during the process step, once important information about video structure is stored inside the header and/or trailer fragments of a video file, depending of the container type. This process can be avoided with a very interesting method. When we refer to split the video, we are actually preparing the data to be distributed in a cluster, and to be processed in parallel. If in the split step, instead of breaking the video file, we just identify the beginning and end points of each chunk, then it would not be necessary to rewrite the container. This greatly reduces the total encoding time. The disadvantage, in this case, is that all nodes must have read access to the original file, which could cause bottlenecks in file reading. Read access can be implemented through a shared file system, as an NFS mount, or even through a distributed file system with high read throughput. The structure bellow exemplifies the output in this split through video marking, which is a data structure containing the chunk marks:

```
[{ 'TYPE' => 'video', 'WIDTH' => output_video_width,
'HEIGHT' => output_video_height, 'CHUNK_START' =>
start_chunk_time, 'CHUNK_END' => end_chunk_time, 'CHUN-
K_ID' => chunk_index, 'ORIGINAL_INPUT_FILE' =>
input_video_filename}]
```

4.1.2 The Process Step

Once the video is fragmented, the chunks generated should be distributed among the nodes to be processed. In the specific case of video compression, this process aims at reducing the size of the video file by eliminating redundancies. In this step, a compression algorithm is applied to each chunk, resulting in a compressed portion of the original video.

The process of chunk encoding is exactly equal to what would be done if the original video was processed without fragmentation, i.e. it is independent of the split and the amount of chunks generated. However, if the option to mark the points of beginning and end of chunks was used during the split, then the processing step should also have read access to all the original video, and must seek to the position of the start frame, and stop the process when the frame that indicates the end of the chunk is achieved. Using this marking approach in the split step, the processing step could be simply implemented as exemplified by the following mencoder [19] command and detailed by Table 4.1:

```
mencoder

   – ofps 30000/1001
   – vf crop=${WIDTH}:${HEIGHT},scale=480:360,harddup

${ORIGINAL_INPUT_FILE}

   – ss ${CHUNK_START}
```

```
- endpos ${CHUNK_END}
- sws 2
- of lavf
- lavfopts
```

format=mp4,i_certify_that_my_video_stream_does_not_use_
b_frames -ovc x264

```
- x264encopts
```

psnr:bitrate=280:qcomp=0.6:qp_min=10:qp_max=51:qp_
step=4:vbv_maxrate=500:vbv_bufsize=2000:level_idc=30:
dct_decimate:me=umh:me_range=16:keyint=250:keyint_min
=25:nofast_pskip:global_header:nocabac:direct_pred=
auto:nomixed_refs:trellis=1:bframes=0:threads=auto:
frameref=1:subq=6

```
- nosound-o $(printf %04u ${CHUNK_ID}).mp4
```

There are several open source tools for video compression, among the most popular, ffmpeg [18, 20] and mencoder [19], which are compatible with various implementations of audio and video codecs. It is possible, for example, to use mencoder to implement the processing step, performing a compression of a high-definition video, generating an output that can be viewed on the Internet, as well as on mobile devices that provide UMTS [21] or HSDPA [22] connectivity. In this case, could be used the H.264 Baseline Profile with 280 kbps, and a 480×360 resolution, performing, therefore, an aspect ratio adjustment.

In addition to processing the video chunks, it is also necessary to process the audio stream, which must be done separately during the split step. Audio compression is a simple process, with a low computational cost. The following piece of code exemplifies the audio processing, and Table 4.2 details it:

```
mencoder
- ${ORIGINAL_INPUT_FILE}
- ovc raw
- ofps 30000/1001
- oac mp3lame
- af lavcresample=22050,channels=1
- lameopts cbr:br=32
- of rawaudio -o audio.mp3
```

At the end of the processing step, video chunks are compressed, as well as the audio stream. To obtain the desired output, we must merge and synchronize all fragments, thus reconstructing the original content in a compressed format.

Table 4.1 Description of MEncoder parameters used for video chunk encoding

Parameter	Description	Used value
ofps	*Output frames per second.* Is the frame rate of the output video	29.97 (the same frame rate of the input)
vf	*Video filters.* A sequence of filters applied before the encoding. (e.g. crop, scale, harddup, etc.)	Original video is firstly cropped to get the 4:3 aspect ratio. Then it is scaled to 480×360 spatial resolution. Finally it is submitted to the harddup filter which writes every frame (even duplicate ones) in the output in order to maintain a/v syncronization
ss	Seek to a position in seconds	This value is set to the chunk start time, extracted in the split step
endpos	Total time to process	This value is set to the chunk end time, extracted in the split step
sws	*Software scaler type.* This option sets the quality (and speed, respectively) of the software scaler	2 (bicubic)
of	*Output format.* Encode output to the specified format	lavf
lavopts	Options for the lavf output format	Format option sets container to mp4. The i_certify_that_my_ video_stream_does_not_use_b_frames explicitly defines that the input and ouput video do not present b-frames. The output video codec is set to x264, an implmentation of H.264
x264encopts	Options for the x264 codec (e.g. bitrate, quantization limits, key frame interval, motion estimation algorithm and range, among others)	In this example the output video bitrate is set to 280 kbps, the GOP size is set to 250 frames, with minimum size of 25 frames, the H.264 profile is set to Baseline with no b-frames
nosound	Discard sound in the encoding process	–

Table 4.2 Description of MEncoder parameters used for audio encoding

Parameter	Description	Used value
ofps	*Output frames per second.* Is the frame rate of the output video	29.97 (30000/1001)
ovc	*Ouput video codec.* Set the codec used in video encoding	The output video codec is set to raw since in this task only audio is considered
oac	*Output audio codec*: Set the codec used in audio encoding	The Lame codec is used to generate an MP3 audio stream
af	*Audio format.* Sets the audio sampling rate, channels, and others	The audio sampling rate is set to 22050 Hz, and the stream has only one channel (mono)
lameopts	Options for the Lame codec	The encoder is set for constant bitrate with an average of 32 kbps of data rate
of	*Output format.* Encode output to the specified format	Rawaudio

4.1.3 The Merge Step

The merge step presents a very interesting challenge, which consists of reconstructing the original content from its parts, so that the fragmentation process is entirely transparent to the end user. Not only the join of the video fragments should be perfect, but also that the audio and video must be fully synchronized. Note that the audio stream was separated from the video before the fragmentation process took place. As compression does not affect the length of the content, in theory after merging the processed chunks, we just need to realign the streams through content mixing.

The first phase of the merge step is to join the chunks of processed video. That can be accomplished easily by ordering the fragments and rewriting the video container. As result, we will have the full compressed video stream, with the same logical sequence of the input. It is done by the identification of chunk index and ordering according to the split order reference, generated at the split step. Using the marking method in the split step, it is not necessary to remove duplicated keyframes, which could appear as consequence of imprecise split that occurs when using some encoding tools where the seek process is based only in timestamp, and not in frame counting, as mencoder, for example. The merge process can be performed using the following operation:

```
mencoder

  - ${LIST_OF_VIDEO_CHUNKS}
  - ovc copy
  - nosound
  - of lavf
  - lavfopts

format=mp4,i_certify_that_my_
video_stream_does_not_use_b_frames
```

```
- o video.mp4
```

Following, we remix the audio stream with the video, synchronizing the contents, and generating the expected output. The remix reconstructs the container by realigning the audio stream with the video stream, and, because the duration of either stream does not change in the compression process, the video content is synchronized in the end.

```
mencoder
    - video.mp4
    - audio-demuxer lavf
    - audiofile audio.mp3
    - ovc copy
    - oac copy
    - of lavf
    - lavfopts

format=mp4,i_certify_that_my_
video_stream_does_not_use_b_frames

    - o ${OUTPUT}
```

The combination of the split, process and merge steps, implemented using the proposed architecture, results in a fully parallel and distributed video compression process, where different pieces of content can be simultaneously processed in either a cluster or, alternatively, in a Cloud infrastructure.

4.2 Deployment in the AWS Cloud

In cases where there is a floating demand or services, or when sudden changes to the environment dictate the need for additional resources, the use of public Cloud Computing platforms to launch applications developed using the Split&Merge architecture becomes extremely interesting. The "pay-as-you-go" business model provides a series of advantages: there are no fixed costs, no depreciation, and it does not require a high initial investment. Furthermore, it is totally elastic, i.e., it is possible to add and remove workers at any time, according to demand. If there is no demand, all workers can be turned off, on the fly, by the master node. Operation costs are thus minimal. Even master nodes may be disconnected, and re-connected, manually, which makes the total cost of operation in idle situations very low. In Fig. 4.4, we illustrate the Split&Merge architecture when used to implement a software application that makes use of a public Cloud infrastructure. Because we opted for the Amazon Web Services (AWS) infrastructure for our experiments, the examples used throughout the text refer to their services. The Split&Merge architecture, however, is general enough to accommodate other choices of cloud service providers.

Fig. 4.4 Split&Merge
architecture deployed on
Amazon Web Services
infrastructure

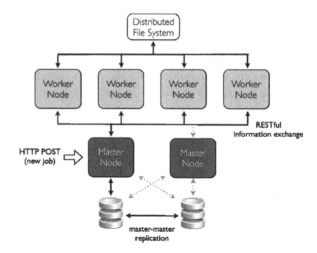

To enable the use of AWS to deploy applications using of the proposed architecture, we first need to build an image (AMI) for EC2 instances, one that corresponds to one full installed and configured worker. This way we ensure that new instances can be started in a state of readiness. We also need a separate image for the master node, because it has different software requirements, since it does not perform the video encoding itself.

For our storage needs, we use Amazon S3. In this case, redundancy and availability concerns are transparent and delegated to the Cloud provider. We also use Amazon Relational Database Service, a service that implements a simple relational database, used, in our architecture, to store the processing state (e.g. which chunks are already processed, which is processing phase, which nodes are available, queue control, among others).

An important point to consider when making a deployment in a public Cloud service, is data delivery and recovery in the Cloud storage. It is relevant because, in addition to paying for data transfer, the network throughput is limited by bandwidth availability between the destination and origin. This factor can greatly impact the performance of the application in question.

4.3 Fault Tolerance Aspects

To understand how the Split&Merge architecture deals with possible failures in its components, we need to detail the implementation of redundancy mechanisms, component behavior, and information exchange. The first point is the way in which messages are exchanged. We advocate in favor of a service-oriented architecture, based on exchange of messages through REST [15] web services.

The typical Map-Reduce [10] implementation [11] provides a single master node, responsible for the scheduling tasks to worker nodes responsible for doing the processing. Communication between workers and the master node is bidirectional: the master node delegates tasks to workers, and the workers post the execution status to the master. This type of architecture has received severe criticism, as a single failure can result in the collapse of the entire system. Conversely, worker failures could happen without ever being detected.

The Split&Merge architecture tackles this problem by coupling a service to the master node, that periodically checks the conditions of its workers. This ensures that the master node, which controls the entire distribution of tasks, is always able to identify whether a node is healthy or not. This simple mechanism can be further refined as necessary, e.g., adding autonomic features, such as monitoring workers to predict when a particular worker is about to fail, isolating problematic nodes, or rescheduling tasks. Of course, care must be taken to avoid overloading the master node with re-scheduling requests, and additional overhead as the result of the action of recovery and prevention mechanisms.

Another issue addressed by the proposed Split&Merge architecture is related to the fact that in traditional Map-Reduce implementations the master node is a single point of failure. The main challenge in having two active masters is sharing state control between them. More specifically, state control sharing means that, whenever one of the master nodes delegates a task, it must inform its mirror which task has been delegated and to which worker node(s), so that both are able to understand the processing status post from the worker(s). State sharing can be implemented through several approaches, but our choice was to use master replication using a common database. In addition to the simplicity of the chosen state sharing solution, we also secure control state persistence. In case of failure, we may resume processing of the chunks from the last consistent state.

We must also pay attention to how workers read the input and write processing results, which translates to the problem of ensuring file system reliability. In cases where a private cluster is used, we opted for a shared file system, e.g. NFS, HDFS (that uses a distributed architecture) [23], or MogileFS [24]. They seem a natural choice as Distributed file systems, in general, already incorporate efficient redundancy mechanisms. In cases where the Cloud is used, storage redundancy is generally transparent, which greatly simplifies the deployment architecture. However, we must note that data writing and reading delays in Cloud storage systems are significantly higher, and often depend on the quality of the connection among nodes and servers that store content.

4.4 Performance Tests

In order to validate the proposed architecture we experimented using Amazon's AWS services. We deployed an instance application responsible for the encoding of different sequences of videos, evaluating the total time required for the encoding

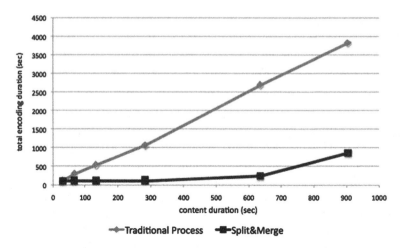

Fig. 4.5 Total encoding times for different sequence durations (in seconds)

process, and comparing it with the total time spent in the traditional process, where the video is encoded without fragmentation, i.e. all content is rendered on a single server.

For these tests, we selected sequences of high-definition video, with different durations, and encoded with MJPEG 25 Mbps, 29.97 fps, and audio PCM/16 Stereo 48 kHz. The video output of the compression process was set to be an H.264 Baseline Profile, with 800 kbps, 29.97 fps, and with a resolution of 854 × 480 (ED), and audio AAC, 64 kbps, Mono 44,100 Hz.

To deploy the infrastructure for this case study, we chose AWS instance types m1.small for all servers. The m1.small type is characterized by the following attributes:

1.7 GB memory
1 EC2 Compute Unit (1 virtual core with 1 EC2 Compute Unit)
160 GB instance storage (150 + 10 GB root partition)
I/O Performance: moderate

In Fig. 4.5 we depict the comparison between total times, measured in seconds, required for the encoding of different video sequences, using the proposed Split&Merge implementation, and using the traditional sequential compression process. In this test scenario, we worked with chunks of fixed size (749 frames), since in MJPEG all frames are key-frames, and with one node per chunk.

Note that, while the total encoding time using the traditional process, grows linearly with increasing duration of the video input, the Split&Merge, average process times remain almost constant for short duration videos. In fact, the total CPU time consumed, which is the sum of the CPU usage in all nodes, will be greater in the Split&Merge approach, however, the distribution of processing among several nodes for parallel execution will reduce the total encoding duration. This result is quite significant when one considers videos of short and average duration. In the case when we have a video about 10 min long, the total time for encoding using the technique of Split&Merge is equivalent to less than 10% of the total time spend using the traditional process, which is extremely interesting for applications where time to market is vital.

Sports coverage can also benefit from a gain in processing time. If we consider the encoding of soccer matches, where videos are typically 2 h long, we could maximize gains by provisioning a greater number of servers in the Cloud. In this case, we are able to reduce the total production time from several hours, to a few minutes. However, as the number of chunks being processed increases, the efficiency of the Split&Merge approach tends to be reduced, as evidenced in Fig. 4.5 (note that there is a significant decay in efficiency for sequences over 700 s long. This fact is explained by network input/output rates, i.e., too many concomitant read operations slow down the process).

Whereas, in the limit, the elastic capacity of a public Cloud tends to exceed user's demand, i.e. the amount of resources available is unlimited (including network latency) from users perspective, then we can say that it is possible to encode all the video content of a production studio collection, with thousands of hours of content, in a few minutes, by using the approach of Split&Merge deployed in a Cloud, which certainly would take hundreds of hours using the traditional process of coding in a private cluster.

4.5 A Cost Analysis

Another point worth considering is the monetary cost of the Split&Merge approach when deployed in a public Cloud infrastructure, against the cost of having a private infrastructure dedicated to this task, with dozens of dedicated servers. Taking into account the results of the tests above, and an average production of 500 min a day, we have, at the end of 1 year, an approximate cost of $25,000 using the Amazon AWS platform, with the added advantage of producing all content in a matter of minutes. This value is comparable to the cost of only one high-end single server, around $20,000 in Brazil, including taxes, not considering the depreciation and maintenance, which makes the architecture of Split&Merge deployed in the public Cloud not only efficient in terms of processing time, but also in terms of deployment and operation costs.

Considering an optimal situation where there are nearly unlimited resources available, it is possible to use the experimental results to predict the total cost and number of nodes needed to encode videos of different categories. Table 4.3 compares the traditional encoding process with the proposed Split&Merge approach. In this example we set the total encoding time to 2 min, and explore several different scenarios, i.e. advertisements, breaking news, TV shows and movies or sports matches, respectively. We base our calculations in the cost per

Table 4.3 Comparison between the traditional encoding process and the Split&Merge approach

Input video duration	Traditional encoding duration	S&M encoding duration (min)	Number of S&M nodes	S&M encoding cost using EC2 (in US$)
30 s	2 min	2	1	$0.003
5 min	19 min	2	10	$0.03
30 min	112 min	2	57	$0.16
2 h	7.5 h	2	225	$0.63

minute, although Amazon's minimum billable timeframe is the hour. We are taking into consideration scenarios where there is a great number of videos to be processed, so machines are up and in use for well over 1 h period.

Note that the Split&Merge approach, when deployed in a public Cloud, reduces the total encoding time for a 2-h video from 7.5 h to 2 min, with the total processing cost of $0.63. If we extrapolate these numbers for the Super Bowl XLIV [25], it is possible to encode the 3.3 h match for $1.03, in only 2 min, as opposed to 12.2 h, if we opted for the traditional process.

Chapter 5
Case Studies

Abstract In order to analyze the Split&Merge efficiency and flexibility, two prototypes were implemented using the architecture deployed in the Amazon Web Services platform. The first one was a video transcoding application used by Globo.com to generate different video formats, for Internet distribution, from a high definition input. The second one was an OCR application for automatic sports video annotation, which detects available information inside video frames and use it to automatically describe the content.

Keywords Video compression · OCR · Split&Merge · Globo.com

In the following sections we present two case studies where the Split&Merge architecture has been successfully used to increase the efficiency of video processing, with focus on reducing the total processing times.

5.1 The Split&Merge for Globo.com Internet Video Compression

Globo.com[1] is the Internet branch of Globo Organizations, the greatest media group of Latin America, and the leader in the broadcasting media segment for the Brazilian internet audiences. As Internet branch, Globo.com is responsible to support all companies from the group in their Internet initiatives. One of the most important of them is making available all content produced for the Globo TV and PayTV channels online. This means that Globo.com needs to produce more than 500 min of video content for the Internet every day. Moreover, all content needs to

---

[1] http://www.globo.com

R. S. Pereira and K. K. Breitman, *Video Processing in the Cloud*,
SpringerBriefs in Computer Science, DOI: 10.1007/978-1-4471-2137-4_5,
© Rafael Silva Pereira 2011

be produced in several different formats, to be consumed by various electronic devices, such computers, laptops, tablets and mobile phones.

For this task, Globo.com developed a video encoding platform, which runs on all content producing sites, such as sports, entertainment and journalism studios. However, with the popularization of the high definition content, the encoding task became much more complex, and the video producing process became a bottleneck, in particular for sports and journalism.

On the sports side, it is Globo.com's responsibility to put on the web all full matches of national soccer tournament, with approximately 2 h of duration each. The problem is that on given Sundays there are 10 simultaneous matches being played and the encoding for one single format takes around 3 h (considering a standard definition input). If the input is in HD, the process is increased to 8 h.

On the journalism side, the problem is with breaking news. With the increase in video quality the time required to make the content available also increases, which is definitely not acceptable for this type of content, that needs to be made available as soon as possible.

Because an increase in production times, both in sports and journalism, was not an option, the solution was to optimize process (aka, encoding) performance. However, since entire video encoding was done in a server, in a straightforward way, the first option to reduce the processing times was to perform a hardware upgrade, replacing the existing infrastructure by most powerful machines. The problem is that even if Globo.com bought the best servers, total encoding times would not be significantly reduced. The demand for peak production times continued to be a problem.

Furthermore, replacing of all encoding hardware would have an outrageous cost, more so if we take into account that the servers would be idle for a great portion of the time. Sports events typically occur during the weekends and there is no way to predict the needs for breaking news. Although feasible, the infrastructure replacement was not a good solution.

Thus, to address this problem efficiently, we implemented a solution using the Split&Merge (S&M) approach proposed in this work. We focused on reducing the total processing time, and the overall cost of the video encoding process, allowing high definition video production without significant increases in the production times. The solution is detailed by the following steps, as shown in Fig. 5.1 as follows.

1. *Content upload to Amazon EC2*. The original content, a DV format video with 25 Mbps of date rate is transferred from Globo.com to Amazon EC2 Master Instance, in a shared filesystem that is mounted by each of EC2 nodes.
2. *Content encoding in EC2 using Split&Merge approach*. After content is transferred from Globo.com to EC2, a message is posted in the EC2 Master Instance, which starts the S&M video encoding, distributing the chunks across several EC2 nodes, which are started or stopped by the Master, according to processing demands.

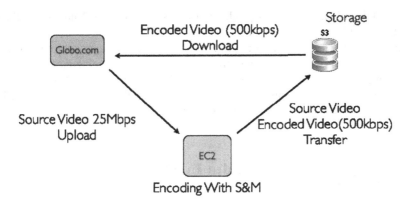

Fig. 5.1 The video production approach using S&M deployed on Amazon AWS

Table 5.1 Cost of S&M approach deployed in Amazon AWS for Globo.com's case

Content upload to Amazon EC2 (DV 25 Mbps)	$9.15
Content encoding in EC2 using Split&Merge approach	$7.58
Original and encoded video transfer from EC2 to S3	$25.23
S3 Storage of original and encoded content	$14.00
Copy of encoded content from S3 to Globo.com	$0.30
Total cost per day (for 500 min of video)	$56.26
Total cost per year	$20,534.90

3. *Original and encoded video transfer from EC2 to S3.* When the encoding process is finished, the compressed video, with 500 kbps of data rate, and the original video, are transferred from the EC2 Master to S3, for permanent storage.
4. *S3 storage of original and encoded content.* The content stored on S3 will remain stored as long as needed, or desired, by Globo.com.
5. *Copy of encoded content from S3 to Globo.com.* Finally, the encoded video is copied to Globo.com, allowing Internet video distribution using the existing infrastructure.

It is possible to calculate to total cost of each step, as well as for the whole process, in order to compare it to the alternative of doing an infrastructure upgrade. For this calculation, we considered an average production of 500 min of video per day, and, one video encoding per video produced, which means that only one format is generated in the output. "Table 5.1, above, shows a detailed analysis"

It is interesting to note that the total processing cost using this approach in an entire year is less than the cost of a single server, without considering the costs associated to power, cooling, maintenance, operations, security and other. This result means that the proposed approach is 100 times, or more, cheaper than the infrastructure upgrade, since the encoding farm has more than 100 servers.

Furthermore, if a new format needs to be produced, for the same original content, the total cost will increase only by $1.00 per day for each additional format, and without increasing production times, as more EC2 nodes for chunk encoding could be engaged as needed.

These results show us that the proposed Split&Merge approach, deployed in Amazon Web Services (AWS) platform, works towards reducing costs as well as processing times for Internet video encoding. However, as a general video processing architecture, it could be used for several different video processing applications, as we exemplify in the next section.

5.2 The Split&Merge for Video Event Extraction Using OCR

The ability to automatically extract information about events in sports videos, e.g. the moment when one team scores a goal, faults, player exchange, as well as additional information such as team, player and stadium names, is extremely interesting in situations where no additional data or is associated with the video. This information can be employed to make useful annotations that can help improve indexing, storing, retrieval and correlating video files for future use.

Usually, the process of video data extraction is done manually, where each video is watched and annotated according to the data seen by a person. However, data extraction and annotation of large amounts of video makes this process slow and costly, and, in many cases, it may turn it unfeasible. Therefore, developing algorithms that can (partly) reproduce the human capacity to extract and classify information is extremely relevant.

Sports videos are very good candidates for automatic information extraction because there is often several bits of relevant information on the video itself. Figure 5.2 exemplifies a video frame that contains information that can be identified and extracted for content annotation. However, to obtain satisfactory results, it is necessary to apply several image-processing techniques for character recognition, to each individual frame, making this task a very complex one.

We would like to call attention to the fact that video and image processing are computationally very expensive processes, i.e., they require a great amount of processing power, as well as large storage resources. Solutions to reduce processing times, and improving the rational use of available resources are thus very important. Motivated by this scenario, we experimented with the Split&Merge approach to extract events from sports videos automatically. Our goal is to make it a timely and efficient process, by using dynamic resource provisioning provided by Cloud services. This represents a huge competitive advantage because, unlike the traditional process, it is possible to process very large videos, that would typically take several hours to process, within minutes (a fixed amount of minutes, for that matter).

To implement this project we made use of different supporting technologies, that had to be combined and extended to obtain the desired goal.

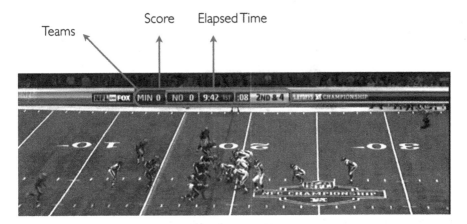

Fig. 5.2 Information inside a sports video

Because development and improvement of OCR algorithms is not the focus of this study, we used a combination of existing tools to perform the character recognition tasks. We chose a well-known, free optical character recognition engine, Tesseract [26], which provides character accuracy greater than 97% [27], and is currently developed by Google. We combined it to ImageMagick [28], a tool that pre processes video frames, cropping out irrelevant information, and transforming the video frame to monochrome with white background, to increase OCR efficiency.

In addition, to allow for the parallel and distributed processing of video frames across multiple nodes, we used CloudCrowd [29], a Ruby framework that implements a scheduler that delegates tasks to different nodes, and obtains the status from them. This tool was used to implement a queue controller responsible for scheduling tasks in a distributed environment.

Finally, to allow for the implementation of an elastic architecture, capable of scaling up according to demand, and being deployed in a public Cloud service, we used the Spit&Merge architecture on to of AWS platform [8, 9] that served as the Cloud infrastructure provider. It is important to note that, in addition to providing processing resources on demand, the AWS platform also provided distributed and fault-tolerant storage as well as a relational database service.

We begin by detailing the sampling technique used for reducing processing times, implemented using the Split&Merge architecture [30–32], as illustrated in Fig. 5.3.

In order to eliminate redundant information, and significantly reduce the amount of information to be processed, we sampled some video frames. Sampling is only possible in situations where the difference of information between subsequent frames is minimal. In the case of sports videos, at 30 frames per second, we extracted only one frame per second, which proved enough to identify the desired information. Then, each sampled video frame was processed. When relevant information was identified, we applied OCR techniques. As a result, for each

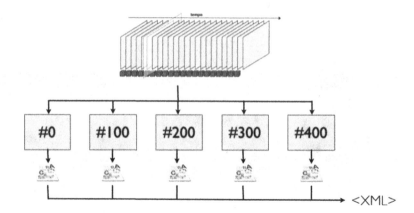

Fig. 5.3 The Split&Merge for video event extraction using OCR

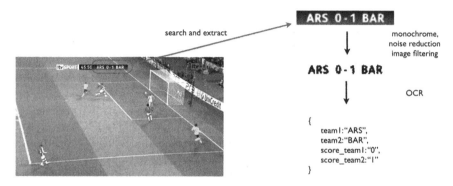

Fig. 5.4 Data extraction process

individual video frame, we extracted a certain amount of information (e.g. the teams, score, elapsed time, among others), as shown in Fig. 5.4.

For the initial tests we selected five different sequences of high-definition 720 p soccer videos, from different matches and with different duration, encoded with MJPEG 30 Mbps, 29.97 fps, and audio PCM/16 Stereo 48 kHz. In these videos, we wanted to identify which were the teams involved in the match, what the final score was, and when a goal was scored. We also wanted to discover which was the sample frequency that offered the best cost-benefit in terms of precision and time required for identification.

For a more realistic scenario, the videos were chosen from different matches, and with short (2 min or less) and long (10 or more minutes) durations. In addition, the score did not appear throughout the content duration, being displayed only at certain moments. About the OCR engine, we use Tesseract 3 without any training, only with a specific dictionary containing each possible acronym for a team.

Fig. 5.5 Efficiency in the
extraction process for
different sampling rates

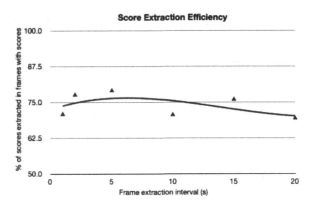

To validate the impact of sampling on processing time and accuracy, each video
was processed several times, each time with a different sampling rate: one with one
frame every 1 s, one frame every 2 s, every 5, 10, 15, 20 and 30 s, so that, the
smaller is the sampling interval, the greater is the amount of frames to be analyzed.

Figure 5.5 shows how the sampling rate influences the efficiency of the
extraction, i.e., the algorithm's capacity to identify and extract a score in a frame
where the score is displayed. Frames without a score were not taken into account.

Note that the extraction efficiency is around 75%, independently of the sampling rate. That is to say that three scores are successfully extracted on each four
occurrences. For example, in a 2-min video, sampling one frame every second,
there are 120 frames to analyze. If 100 frames of the 120 have some score displayed, the proposed algorithm can extract 75 scores from these frames, i.e., in 75
frames the OCR process returns relevant information. Also note that increasing the
sampling interval, the extraction efficiency suffers a slight reduction, and it could
be a consequence of the small number of frames to analyze. In fact, the extraction
efficiency should not present great variations when using different sampling rates,
since each frame is isolated processed.

On the other hand, the algorithm's capacity to extract the information correctly
is directly related to the number of frames analyzed. With more frames, the greater
will be the information available to make a better decision. With lower information volume, the extraction becomes guessing, as the algorithm chooses the highest
probability option.

As expected, Fig. 5.6 shows that with lower frame sampling intervals the
probability of correct score identification increases, and stabilizes around 87%.
This result means that in 87% of extracted scores, the output of OCR process is
correct, which is directly consistent with Tesseract's engine efficiency. This value,
in fact, is obtained for one isolated frame, an not for the full video analysis. This
means that the efficiency of a video data extraction could be greater if we consider
a hole set of frames and use them to perform a correction in eventual identification
errors. It is also important to remind that some OCR tools, such as Tesseract,

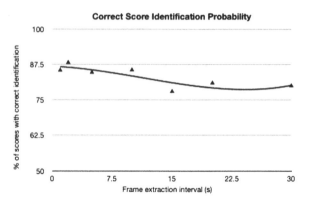

Fig. 5.6 The probability of a correct identification by the OCR engine

could be trained to increase the efficiency in the OCR process, and, in this first prototype, we didn't perform such training.

One important remark is that, since the desired extraction output is the name of teams in the match, the final score, and the name of the team that scored the goal, obtained through a composition of all OCR outputs, for this test set and for all tested sampling rates the returned information is correct.

To demonstrate the advantages brought forth by the proposed architecture we compare the cloud implementation to results using the traditional process (process all frames in a single server). Figure 5.7 shows the times, measured in seconds, required for the processing of different number of frames, with always one worker per frame (in the cloud environment), using the proposed Split&Merge implementation (darker line), and the ones using the traditional process (gray line).

Note that the Split&Merge implementation requires only 30% of the total time spent using the traditional process, which is extremely interesting for applications where time-to-market is vital. Indeed, as neither the split nor the merge steps can be parallelized, its execution time will be independent of the amount of active workers, and will be responsible for the increasing in processing time for the Split&Merge approach.

To provide an idea of cost savings, we contrast the Split&Merge approach when deployed in the public Cloud, against the costs of having a private infrastructure dedicated to this task. Taking into account the results presented in Fig. 5.7, we have an approximate cost of $0.0007 per minute of video, considering a 1 s sampling interval, to get the results three times faster, using the Amazon AWS platform, with the additional advantage that it is possible to process very large videos in a few seconds. The total cost shows that the architecture of Split&Merge deployed in the public Cloud is not only efficient in terms of processing time, but also in deployment and operation costs.

Considering an optimal situation where there are unlimited resources available, it is possible to use the experimental results to predict the total cost and number of nodes needed to process videos of different durations. Table 5.2, compares the

Fig. 5.7 Total processing times for different number of workers

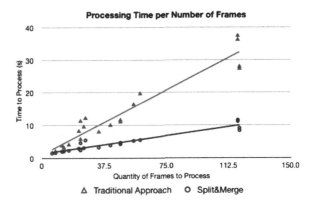

Table 5.2 Comparison between the traditional process and the Split&Merge approach, for 1 s of sampling interval

Input video duration	Traditional process duration	S&M process duration	Number of S&M nodes	Normalized S&M cost using EC2 (in US dollar)
30 s	9 s	3 s	30	$0.0003
5 min	9 min	2 min	300	$0.005
30 min	53 min	13 min	1,800	$0.029
2 h	3.5 h	41 min	7,200	$0.103

traditional process with the proposed S&M approach. In this example the goal is to get the total process time five times faster using S&M. We are also using the cost per minute, although Amazon's minimum timeframe is one full hour, considering scenarios where there are a great number of videos to be processed, so, that machines are not shut down after a single process.

Note that the Split&Merge approach, deployed in a public Cloud, reduces the total processing time for a 2-h video from 3.5 h to 41 min, with the total processing cost of $0.103. However, it is possible to instantiate more workers, reducing the total processing time even more, to just a few seconds, and for the exact same price. In this case, the total reduction in processing time will be limited to the necessary time to perform the split and the merge steps.

Chapter 6
Limitations

Abstract After prototypes implementation and performance evaluation, it is possible to highlight some bottlenecks that could reduce the architecture efficiency, and some limitations that restrict its usage. In this chapter we discuss how the network, inside and outside the Cloud platform, the architecture itself, and the Cloud platforms heterogeneity, could reduce the Split&Merge efficiency or even restricts its usage.

Keywords Cloud computing · Split&Merge · Networks · Cloud platforms

After prototypes implementation and performance evaluation, it is possible to highlight some bottlenecks that could reduce the architecture efficiency, and some limitations that restrict its usage. It is also possible to identify some improvement aspects that could be addressed in further researches, focusing in increase reliability and scalability of the proposed architecture.

One of the main limitations of the Split&Merge architecture, when deployed in the Cloud, is the bandwidth availability between the Cloud platform and the content owner. In fact, this limitation is not directly related with the architecture itself, but, in some cases, it could turn the chosen for public cloud unfeasible. In the scenario in which our tests were performed, this bandwidth issue was impeditive for the adoption of proposed approach in the Globo.com video compression case.

In fact, since the high resolution video, with high data rates, must be uploaded into the Cloud, this approach requires a really high bandwidth availability between the server were content is stored and the virtual machine in the Cloud in which videos will be processed. Ideally the bandwidth should be at least four times greater than content data rate, adding only 25% of content duration of overhead in the total time required to obtain the encoded video. As shown in Fig. 5.1 of Sect. 5.1, in the Globo.com case, these high definition videos must be transferred from Globo.com's datacenter to Amazon AWS platform, using the public internet

R. S. Pereira and K. K. Breitman, *Video Processing in the Cloud*,
SpringerBriefs in Computer Science, DOI: 10.1007/978-1-4471-2137-4_6,
© Rafael Silva Pereira 2011

links for this task. In this specific case, the Globo.com's datacenter is in Brazil, and should send videos to Amazon's cloud platform in US, using intercontinental pipes which are frequently overloaded, and where it is not possible to reach even the 25 Mbps of data rate used in the original videos. In this scenario, the overall time required to get the encoded content is higher than if the content is processed using the traditional approach, which basically discards all encoding gains obtained by the Split&Merge architecture itself, due to network limitations.

However, the scope of this limitation is restricted to this usage scenario. If the architecture was deployed in a private cloud, inside the content owner's datacenter, or if there is a high bandwidth availability between the Cloud and the content owner, for example, using a dedicated and/or a private link, this network bottleneck could be removed, and all benefits of Split&Merge could be really obtained. Furthermore, the telecommunications infrastructure is constantly evolving, frequently increasing the network capacity. These investments basically means that this will not be an issue anymore in the next few years, and the architecture would be deployed and used as proposed.

Besides this network bottleneck, there is another limitation that could impact in the overall architecture performance, and it is related specifically with the split and the merge steps. In the way which architecture was conceived, all operations of the split and the merge steps were executed sequentially by one single sever (or virtual machine in the Cloud deploy). This means that if the split or the merge steps were complex, with a high computational cost, the performance of process will be reduced.

In the both cases analyzed in previous section, the computational cost of split and merge is directly associated with the input size. For video compression, longer the video, more chunks will be generated, more computational cost will be required to seek, calculate and find chunks. In this case, longer inputs will result in an increased duration of the split step. The same analysis works for the merge step. With more chunks, a longer video stream will be produced, and more computational cost will be needed to order, synchronize and remix the content.

In this approach, performing the split an the merge steps in one single server, as more complex are the performed operations to fragment the input and to combine them to get the output, more the performance will be impacted and lower will be the benefits obtained by the Split&Merge approach. In fact, better results will be obtained for simple split and merge tasks, and complex chunk processing.

Another identified limitation appears when the Split&Merge is deployed in public clouds. As a network bottleneck could be found outside the Cloud infrastructure, when uploading the content, another network issue could degrade the architecture performance, but, this time, inside the Cloud.

During the process step, a master node continuously communicate with the worker nodes, to obtain the processing status, to delegate new tasks, and to perform failover controls, retrieving the state of each node. Working with the approach of one node by each chunk, one can have hundreds or even thousands of working nodes, running in the same Cloud infrastructure. In the limit, the internal network of the Cloud platform will be overloaded by the messages exchanged between the architecture's virtual machines, which basically could stop all content processing. A good approach to tackle these bottlenecks is to constantly monitor the network path between the nodes, controlling overloads by shutting virtual machines down. In this case, having less nodes then chunks could be the best alternative to not increase significantly the time required to obtain the desired results.

Finally, the last important limitation is related with the heterogeneity of public Cloud platforms. When deploying the Split&Merge in a public Cloud environment, one has to perform several customizations to use the API services provided by the platform to allow resources administration. This basically means that each service provider has its proprietary API to, for example, start and stop virtual machines, or to store and retrieve contents from the storage. Deploying the architecture in a different Cloud platform usually means that all interfaces to perform these simple tasks must be rewritten in the application side, which, in some cases, could be really complex and time consuming.

Today there is no standardization of these public APIs to manage the Cloud resources, and, as result, each provider adopts the technologies and formats that fit better in their needs. This problem became even more critical if we consider that each platform uses different authentication/authorization processes, and even different protocols to allow users to perform these basic tasks.

One alternative to address this issue is to build a middleware that is capable to abstract the Cloud platform interfaces from the applications development, and which is maintained by the service providers themselves. In this scenario, the Cloud platforms will became responsible to develop and maintain a common interface for developers to perform this basic set of operations, such start and stop servers.

With this approach, the choice between one Cloud platform and other could be performed at runtime, using the provider with better quality of service at that specific moment, since, by the application point of view, the operations for servers administration will be the same, independent of who is providing the service. Other service providers, such that in the telecommunications area, already do this same approach, abstracting from the device manufacturers the differences between their infrastructures.

Chapter 7
Conclusions

The need for systems that can deal efficiently with increasingly large volumes of information, is growing at an astounding pace. New architectures and techniques to optimize the use of available resources are an important part of today's research agenda. The emergence and subsequent evolution of services in the Cloud, provide the necessary flexibility and makes the task of processing of large datasets more accessible and scalable, especially in scenarios with varying demand.

Today there are various solutions geared towards the optimization of computer resource usage, and performance improvement in information processing. Among them, we highlight the Map-Reduce paradigm, firstly proposed as a solution to optimize web searches. We understand, however, that it requires some adaptation if it is to be used efficiently in other domains. In *Video Processing in the Cloud* we proposed a generalization of the Map-Reduce paradigm, adapted and finely tuned to deal with video compression. We proposed a more efficient architecture than the original one proposed by Dean and Ghemawat [10], that can be deployed both in private clusters, as in commercial Cloud infrastructures. We generalized the Map-Reduce paradigm by proposing the Split&Merge approach, a video processing strategy that allows for the use of multiple video compressing techniques (different for audio and video processing), and provides total control during the reduce step.

It is important to note that the techniques used in both the Split&Merge steps are hotspots, i.e., techniques can be exchanged and customized as needed. That ensures flexibility, adaptation, extensibility and generality to the proposed architecture. In the case of video processing, it is paramount to allow a choice among *codecs*, containers, audio streams, and different splitting techniques. To illustrate one such scenario, let us take the cases where the input video has no temporal compression (MJPEG [16] for example). In such cases, the split operation can be performed at any video frame. Conversely, cases when the input is a video with

R. S. Pereira and K. K. Breitman, *Video Processing in the Cloud*,
SpringerBriefs in Computer Science, DOI: 10.1007/978-1-4471-2137-4_7,
© Rafael Silva Pereira 2011

p-frame only temporal compression (H.264 [17] Baseline Profile for example), it is mandatory to identify key-frames before splitting.

The generalization of this idea, lead to an architecture in which it is possible to isolate, and modify the implementations for the split, process and merge steps. The current implementation encompasses a choice of techniques that range from video compression to image processing, through macroblock fragmentation for simple word counts. This choice can be done at scheduling time, as the current implementation embeds the technique of choice in a web service, at run time.

We also pointed out that the deployment in a private cluster is only justified in situations where there is a constant demand for processing. The alternative, i.e., situations where the demand is seasonal, makes use of a commercial, public cloud platform, such as Amazon, where one pays for the amount of resources used.

We validated the proposed Split&Merge architecture and verified its behavior for processing large volumes of information, both in private clusters and in commercial, public cloud scenarios, by the implementation of the Split&Merge approach for a distributed video compression application. As a result, we were able to dramatically reduce video encoding times. In fact, we demonstrated that if we scale the architecture up to a maximum of one worker per 250 frame chunk, we can guarantee fixed encoding times, independently of the size of the video input. This is extremely interesting for content producers, because it is possible to establish entry independent software level agreements (SLAs) for video encoding services.

We also developed a Split&Merge application for automatic video data extraction using OCR. As result, we obtained a tool capable of extracting basic text information present inside soccer video frames, e.g. the name of the teams, score and elapsed time, which can be used for automatica content annotation. Applications such as this can greatly leverage search and retrieval of legacy video. We also demonstrate that the usage of Split&Merge in this application significantly reduces the time and cost required to perform this process.

7.1 Future Work

The deployment of an application to compress videos in a Cloud, following the proposed architecture, is still something that presents several challenges. The main limiting factor of this approach is, at least in our geographic area, the lack of availability of bandwidth between content producers, and services in the Cloud. For example, using a Cloud service to compress high definition videos for web distribution is prohibitive by today's standards, as the videos to be processed have to be uploaded in their original, high definition, formats. In this particular case, deployment in a private cluster is more efficient in respect to the total production time.

Finally, we believe our architecture could be used in applications other than video processing. Future work includes the experimentation with different datasets, to determine the actual scope of the proposed architecture. Another issue we would like to investigate is the incorporation of autonomic computing mechanisms to help anticipate and identify faults, and the implementation of efficient prevention and recovery mechanisms. That will contribute to making the present solution more robust.

Glossary

API   An application programming interface (API) is an interface implemented by a software program to enable interaction with other software, similar to the way a user interface facilitates interaction between humans and computers

Codec   A codec is a device or computer program capable of encoding and/or decoding a digital data stream or signal. The word codec is a portmanteau (a blending of two or more words) of 'compressor–decompressor' or, more commonly, 'coder–decoder'

DV   DV is a format for recording and playing back digital video. It was launched in 1995 with joint efforts of leading producers of video camera recorders

DCT   "Discrete Cosine Transform", a mathematical transform that can provide aliasing cancellation and good frequency resolution, used in some codecs to convert the audio or video signal from the time domain to the frequency domain

GOP   Group of Pictures, it starts with one I-frame and ends with the next I-frame, excluding the next I-frame

HD   High definition. Usually used to describe any device capable of generating or displaying a signal with a resolution of at least 720 vertical lines (i.e. 720p)

HTML   HTML, which stands for HyperText Markup Language, is the predominant markup language for web pages

HTML 5   HTML5 is being developed as the next major revision of HTML. In particular, HTML5 adds many new syntactical features. These include the *<video>*, *<audio>*, and *<canvas>* elements, as well as

R. S. Pereira and K. K. Breitman, *Video Processing in the Cloud,*
SpringerBriefs in Computer Science, DOI: 10.1007/978-1-4471-2137-4,
© Rafael Silva Pereira 2011

the integration of SVG content. These features are designed to make it easy to include and handle multimedia and graphical content on the web without having to resort to proprietary plugins and APIs

HTTP/   HTTP is an application protocol, which defines how files on the
HTTPS   World Wide Web are transferred. HTTPS (HTTP over SSL or HTTP
            Secure) is the use of Secure Socket Layer (SSL) or Transport Layer
            Security (TLS) as a sublayer under regular HTTP

NFS   Network File System. Standard for accessing files on a remote
            computer appearing as a local volume

OCR   Optical Character Recognition. The technology that allows
            computers to 'read' text from files, such as images

RGB   An additive color model based on red (R), green (G), and blue (B)
            light. RGB is used by computers, televisions, and film recorders to
            display colors

SD   Standard definition. Usually defined as a 480i signal (480 interlaced
            scan lines) presented 30 times per second

SLA   A service level agreement (frequently abbreviated as SLA) is a part
            of a service contract where the level of service is formally defined.
            In practice, the term SLA is sometimes used to refer to the
            contracted delivery time (of the service) or performance

UGC   User-generated content (UGC), also known as consumer-generated
            media (CGM) or user-created content (UCC), refers to various kinds
            of media content, publicly available, that are produced by end-users

References

1. Armbrust, M., Fox, M., Griffith, R., et al.: Above the clouds: a Berkeley view of cloud computing. University of California at Berkeley Technical Report no. UCB/EECS-2009-28, pp. 6–7, 10 Feb 2009
2. Vogels, W.: A head in the clouds—the power of infrastructure as a service. First Workshop on Cloud Computing in Applications (CCA'08), October 2008
3. Cloud computing—web-based applications that change the way you work and collaborate online (2009)
4. Vaquero, L.M., Rodero-Merino, L., Caceres, J., Lindner, M.: A break in the clouds: towards a cloud definition. ACM SIGCOMM Comput. Comm. Rev. **39**(1), 50–55 (2009)
5. Danielson, K.: Distinguishing cloud computing from utility computing. Ebizq.net (2008). Accessed 22 Aug 2010
6. Gartner say's cloud computing will be as influential as E-business. Gartner.com. Accessed 22 Aug 2010
7. Gruman, G.: What cloud computing really means. InfoWorld (2008). Accessed 2 June 2009
8. Amazon Elastic Compute Cloud: Developer Guide, API Version 2009-04-04. http://awsdocs. s3.amazonaws.com/EC2/latest/ec2-dg.pdf
9. Amazon EC2: Instances. http://aws.amazon.com/ec2/#instance
10. Dean, J., Ghemawat, S.: MapReduce: simplified data processing on large clusters. OSDI (2004)
11. Apache Hadoop. http://hadoop.apache.org/mapreduce/
12. Lane, T.G.: Advanced features: compression parameter selection. Using the IJG JPEG Library. http://apodeline.free.fr/DOC/libjpeg/libjpeg-3.htm
13. Enomoto, H., Shibata, K.: Features of Hadamard transformed television signal. Presented at the National Conference IECE in Japan. Paper 881 (1965)
14. Andrews, H.C., Pratt, W.K.: Fourier transform coding of images. In: Proceedings of Hawaii International Conference System Sciences, pp. 677–679 (1968)
15. Zhang, L.: RESTful Web Services. Web Services, Architecture Seminar, University of Helsink, Department of Computer Science (2004)
16. Symes, P.: Video Compression. McGraw-Hill, New York (1998)
17. Information technology—Coding of audio–visual objects—Part 10: Advanced Video Coding, ISO/IEC 14496-10:2003. http://www.iso.org/iso/iso_catalogue/catalogue_ics/catalogue_ detail_ics.html?csnumber=37729
18. FFMpeg. http://ffmpeg.org
19. MEncoder. http://www.mplayerhq.hu
20. Converting video formats with FFMpeg, Linux J. Arch. (146), 10 (2006)

R. S. Pereira and K. K. Breitman, *Video Processing in the Cloud*,
SpringerBriefs in Computer Science, DOI: 10.1007/978-1-4471-2137-4,
© Rafael Silva Pereira 2011

21. Ganesh, R., Pahlavan, K., Zvonar, Z.: UMTS/IMT-2000 standardization. Wireless Multimedia Network Technologies, vol. 524, pp. 75–93. Springer, US (1999)
22. Harri, H., Antti, T.: HSDPA/HSUPA for UMTS: high speed radio access for mobile communications. Willey, New York (2006)
23. Hadoop Distributed File System. http://hadoop.apache.com/hdfs/
24. MogileFS. http://www.danga.com/mogilefs
25. SuperBowl Stats "STLtoday.com—Sports—Stats, Inc". http://stltoday.stats.com/fb/boxscore.asp?gamecode=20100207011&home=11&vis=18&final=true. Accessed 2 Sept 2010
26. Tesseract. http://code.google.com/p/tesseract-ocr/
27. Rice, S.V., Jenkins, F.R., Nartker, T.A.: The Fourth Annual Test of OCR Accuracy. http://www.isri.unlv.edu/downloads/AT-1995.pdf
28. ImageMagick. http://www.imagemagick.org
29. CloudCrowd. http://wiki.github.com/documentcloud/cloud-crowd/getting-started
30. Pereira, R., Azambuja, M., Breitman, K., Endler, M.: An architecture for distributed high performance video processing. IEEE Cloud Conference, Miami, Fl, July 2010
31. Pereira, R., Azambuja, M., Breitman, K., Endler, M.: When TV dies will it go to the cloud? IEEE Comput. Mag. **43**, 81–83 (2010)
32. Pereira, R., Azambuja, M., Breitman, K., Endler, M.: Architectures for distributed video processing in the cloud—CloudSlam, April 2010
33. Vanam, R., Riskin, E.A., Ladner, R.E.: H.264/MPEG-4 AVC Encoder Parameter Selection Algorithms for Complexity Distortion Tradeoff, Data Compression Conference, 2009. DCC '09, pp. 372–381, 16–18 March 2009
34. Jiang, W., Liu, W., Latecki, L.J., Liang, H., Wang, C., Feng, B.: Two-Step Coding for High Definition Video Compression, Data Compression Conference (DCC), 2010, pp. 535–535, 24–26 March 2010
35. Chen, H.H., Huang, Y.-H., Su P.-Y., Ou, T.-S.: Improving video coding quality by perceptual rate-distortion optimization, Multimedia and Expo (ICME), 2010 IEEE International Conference, pp. 1287–1292, 19–23 July 2010
36. Teng, C.-Y.: An improved block prediction mode for H.264/AVC intra-frame prediction, Data Compression Conference, 2004. Proceedings. DCC 2004, p. 569, 23–25 March 2004
37. Ahmed, N., Natarajan, T., Rao, K.R.: On image processing and a discrete cosine transform. IEEE Trans. Comput. **C-23**(1), 90–93 (1974)
38. Hyperconnectivity and the Approaching Zettabyte Era, Cisco Systems. http://www.cisco.com/en/US/solutions/collateral/ns341/ns525/ns537/ns705/ns827/VNI_Hyperconnectivity_WP.html. June 2010
39. Akamai State of Internet Report. http://www.akamai.com/stateoftheinternet
40. American National Standards Institute (ANSI). T1.413-1998 Network and Customer Installation Interfaces—Asymmetric Digital Subscriber Line (ADSL) Metallic Interface (1998)
41. HTML 5 Draft. http://dev.w3.org/html5/spec/Overview.html. March 2011
42. Lawton, G.: Developing software online with platform-as-a-service technology. IEEE Comput. **41**, 13–15 (2008)
43. Types of PaaS Solutions. http://www.salesforce.com/paas/paas-solutions/
44. Map Reduce. http://map-reduce.wikispaces.asu.edu
45. Tan, J., Pan, X., Marinelli, E., Kavulya, S., Gandhi, R., Narasimhan, P.: Kahuna: Problem diagnosis for Mapreduce-based cloud computing environments. Network Operations and Management Symposium (NOMS), 2010 IEEE
46. Snell, J., Tidwell, D., Kulchenko, P.: Programming Web Services with SOAP. O'Reilly Media (2001)
47. Amazon AMIs. http://aws.amazon.com/amis
48. Murty, J.: Programming Amazon Web Services: S3, EC2, SQS, FPS, and SimpleDB. O'Reilly Media (2008)

49. Chu, W.W., Holloway, L.J., Lan M.-T., Efe, K.: Task allocation in distributed data processing. IEEE Comput. **13**, 57–69 (1980)
50. Hwang K.: Advanced parallel processing with supercomputer architectures. Proc. IEEE **75**, 1348–1379 (1987)
51. Feitelson, D.G., Rudolph, L.: Distributed hierarchical control for parallel processing. IEEE Comput. **23**, 65–70 (1990)
52. Huffman, D.A.: A Method for the construction of minimum-redundancy codes. Proc. I.R.E. **40**, 1098–1102 (1952)
53. Welch, T.: A technique for high-performance data compression. IEEE Comp. **17**, 8–19 (1984)
54. Ziv, J., Lempel, A.: Compression of individual sequences via variable-rate coding. IEEE Trans. Inf. Theory **24**, 530–536 (1978)
55. Foreman Video Sequence. http://ise.stanford.edu/Video/foreman.qcif.gz
56. MPEG-2 ISO/IEC 13818. http://www.iso.org/iso/en/CatalogueDetailPage.CatalogueDetail? CSNUMBER=31537
57. ITU-T: H.263: Video coding for low bit rate communication. http://www.itu.int/rec/T-REC-H.263/
58. ISO. "ISO/IEC 14496-2:2004—Information technology—Coding of audio–visual objects— Part 2: Visual". http://www.iso.org/iso/iso_catalogue/catalogue_ics/catalogue_detail_ics. htm?csnumber=39259
59. Sorenson Spark Codec. http://www.sorenson.com/
60. Macromedia and sorenson media bring video to macromedia flash content and applications. http://www.adobe.com/macromedia/proom/pr/2002/flash_mx_video.html
61. Zhang, Q., Cheng, L., Boutaba, R.: Cloud computing: state-of-the-art and research challenges. J. Internet Servi. Appl. (JISA) **1**(1), 7–18 (2010) (Springer, London)
62. Demystifying SaaS, PaaS and IaaS. http://e2enetworks.com/2010/05/03/demystifying-saas-paas-and-iaas/
63. Wallace, G.K.: The JPEG still picture compression standard. IEEE Trans. Consumer Electron. **38**, 18–34 (1991)
64. Information technology—Digital compression and coding of continuous-tone still images: Requirements and guidelines, ISO/IEC 10918-1:1994. http://www.iso.org/iso/iso_catalogue/catalogue_tc/catalogue_detail.htm?csnumber=18902
65. JPEG. http://en.wikipedia.org/wiki/JPEG
66. Anttila, I., Paakkunainen, M.: Transferring real-time video on the Internet, Helsinki University of Technology, Telecommunications Software and Multimedia Laboratory. http://www.tml.tkk.fi/Opinnot/Tik-110.551/1997/iwsem.html
67. T.802 : Information technology—JPEG 2000 image coding system: Motion JPEG 2000. http://www.itu.int/rec/T-REC-T.802/en
68. VP8 Data Format and Decoding Guide—IETF. http://tools.ietf.org/html/draft-bankoski-vp8-bitstream-01
69. MPEG-4 AVC/H.264 Video Codecs Comparison, CS MSU Graphics&Media Lab, Video Group. http://www.compression.ru/video/codec_comparison/index_en.html
70. Amazon Simple Storage Service. http://aws.amazon.com/s3/

Index

A
Amazon Machine Images, 9
Amazon Web Services, 8, 37, 42, 44
  cost, 40
  services, 8, 23
    EBS. *See* Elastic Block Storage, 9
    EC2. *See* Elastic Compute
      Cloud, 8, 23, 33
    Elastic Map-Reduce. *See* Elastic
      Map-Reduce, 11
    S3. *See* Simple Storage Service, 8, 34
AMI. *See* Amazon Machine Images, 9
AWS. *See* Amazon Web
    Services, 8, 37, 42, 44

C
Cloud. *See* Cloud Computing, 6
Cloud Computing, 6
  Amazon (AWS). *See* Amazon Web
    Services, 8, 37, 42, 44
  definition, 6
  elasticity, 3
  HaaS. *See* Infrastructure as a Service, 7
  IaaS. *See* Infrastructure as a Service, 7
  layers, 7
  PaaS. *See* Platform as a Service, 7
  SaaS. *See* Software as a Service, 7
CloudCrowd, 43

D
Digital Image, 13
  lossless compression, 16
  lossy compression, 17

  quantization, 17
  structure, 14
Digital Video, 17, 25
  fps, 16
  frame types
  inter compression, 21
  intra compression, 20
  lossless compression, 17
  lossy compression, 17
  motion compensation, 18
Discrete Cosine Transform, 14

E
EBS. *See* Elastic Block Storage, 9
EC2. *See* Elastic Compute Cloud, 8, 23
Elastic Block Storage, 9
Elastic Compute Cloud, 8, 23
  availability zones, 9
  Available APIs, 8
  images. *See* Amazon
    Machine Images, 9
  instance management, 7
  storage, 9
Elastic Map-Reduce, 11

F
Flash Media. *See* Internet Video:
    Flash Media, 20

G
Globo.com, 41, 49
  video processing challenges, 39

R. S. Pereira and K. K. Breitman, *Video Processing in the Cloud*,
SpringerBriefs in Computer Science, DOI: 10.1007/978-1-4471-2137-4,
© Rafael Silva Pereira 2011

H

H.264, 25, 26, 36
HaaS. *See* Infrastructure as a Service, 7
Hadoop, 13
Hardware as a Service. *See* Infrastructure as a
     Service, 7

I

IaaS. *See* Infrastructure as a Service, 7
ImageMagick, 43
Infrastructure as a Service, 7
Internet Video
     distribution, 3, 20
     evolution, 21
     Flash Media, 20
     RealVideo, 19
     Windows Media, 20

J

JPEG Compression, 14

M

Map-Reduce, 11, 25, 26, 35
     limitations
Motion JPEG, 17, 24, 36, 44

O

OCR, 45, 46

P

PaaS. *See* Platform as a Service, 7
Platform as a Service, 7
     types, 7

R

RealVideo. *See* Internet Video:RealVideo, 20

S

S3. *See* Simple Storage Service, 8, 34
SaaS. *See* Software as a Service, 7
Simple Storage Service, 8, 34

access control, 10
available APIs, 11
buckets, 10
objects, 10
redundancy, 10
RRS, 11
Software as a Service, 7
Split&Merge, 25, 27
     applications, 42, 46
     cost, 41, 42, 47
     deployment, 35, 37, 46, 54
     fault tolerance, 35
     limitations, 49
     merge step, 33
          audio remixing, 33
          container reconstruction, 33
          video joining, 32
     performance, 36, 49
     process step, 31
          audio processing, 31
          example command, 29
          video processing, 29
     split step, 28
          algorithm, 29
          challenges, 27
          optimization, 24
          special cases, 28
          time marking method, 32

T

Tesseract, 44, 45
     efficiency, 46
TV Model, 2

U

UGC, 2

V

Virtualization, 7

W

Windows Media. *See* Internet
          Video:Windows Media, 20